Civil Society
**in Question**

*"Civil society is a geographically and socially uneven
landscape. It is and always will be contested terrain."*

# Civil Society
# in Question

## Jamie Swift

between the lines

Between the Lines gratefully acknowledges financial assistance for our publishing activities from the Ontario Arts Council, The Canada Council for the Arts, and the Government of Canada through the Book Publishing Industry Development Program.

Special publishing support for this book was provided by South Asia Partnership, 1 Nicholas Street, Suite 200, Ottawa, Ontario, Canada, K1N 7B7 and by The Trillium Foundation.

Every reasonable effort has been made to find copyright holders. The publisher would be pleased to have any errors or omissions brought to its attention.

**Canadian Cataloguing in Publication Data**

Swift, Jamie, 1951-
      Civil society in question

Published in collaboration with South Asia Partnership Canada.
Includes bibliographic references and index.
ISBN 1-896357-24-5

1. Civil society. 2. Social justice. 3. Economic development—Citizen participation. 4. Voluntarism. I. South Asia Partnership Canada. II. Title.

JC336.S94 1999         301         C99-930378-3

Editor: Robert Clarke
Design: Point of View
Printed in Canada by Transcontinental Printing

1 2 3 4 5 6 7 8 9 10   TP   05 04 03 02 01 00 99 98

Between the Lines
720 Bathurst Street, # 404     (416) 535-9914
Toronto, Ontario             btlbooks@web.net
M5S 2R4, Canada           www.btlbooks.com

THE CANADA COUNCIL | LE CONSEIL DES ARTS
FOR THE ARTS | DU CANADA
SINCE 1957 | DEPUIS 1957

*for Richard and David*

# Contents

# Foreword

by Richard Harmston,
Executive Director, SAP Canada

South Asia Partnership (SAP) is an alliance of six voluntary development organizations in Canada and South Asia that have been working together since 1981 to support sustainable human development in South Asia. The six independent national organizations—SAP Canada, SAP Bangladesh, SAP India, SAP Nepal, SAP Pakistan, and SAP Sri Lanka—constitute SAP International, governed by an international board and co-ordinated through a Secretariat in Colombo, Sri Lanka.

With a shared goal of working towards the elimination of poverty, powerlessness, and injustice in South Asia and globally, the SAP network believes in the potential of people's organizations to bring about lasting change. SAP is dedicated to strengthening the capacities, voices, and collective action of community organizations nationally, throughout the South Asia region, and internationally.

SAP organizations in Asia provide a range of capacity-building services to over one thousand NGOs and community-based organizations in South Asia. Training, networking, community development, communications, and advocacy programs contribute to building strong, self-determined communities that can address local problems, manage development activities, and contribute to public policies on matters affecting people's lives. In addition to their national programs, SAP organizations also work on a regional basis through SAP International, bringing community activists and decision-makers together on regional and global issues.

In Canada, SAP Canada acts as a forum and information centre for a membership of twenty-two NGOs and a broad constituency of diverse organizations interested in human development and justice, specifically in South Asia. SAP Canada members and networks provide support to SAP programs in Asia, participate in learning and solidarity activities with South Asian organizations, and collaborate to increase public engagement and government support for development in South Asia.

Each year, SAP Canada holds a major forum in Canada on an evolving issue related to development work in South Asia. The 1997 forum, "Strengthening Civil Society: Progressive Strategy or Smokescreen?" grew out of an increasing use of the terminology of civil society by SAP and others, and exposure to the brewing debate on civil society as a development strategy.

Why was the term being used? What were donor expectations? Was it distracting from poverty reduction activity? Was it reflecting an abrogation of government responsibilities or an emphasis on the market? Did it offer a more empowering context for development effort? Did it imply new approaches or was it "old wine in a new bottle"?

The forum aimed to generate analysis, country-specific information, donor perspectives, dialogue, reflection, and strategies. Participants explored theoretical concepts of civil society, civil society environments and relations in Canada and South Asia, and civil society as a development strategy; they participated in case studies on strengthening civil society; and they considered the nature of partnerships for civil society.

The forum was organized by SAP in partnership with the International NGO Training and Research Centre (INTRAC—Oxford, U.K.) and the North-South Institute, Ottawa. It was held in three locations across Canada: the International Development Research Centre in Ottawa, the University of

Calgary (with the Division of International Development), and the Coady International Institute in Antigonish, Nova Scotia. Participants in these three events included thirty-eight resource people from Canada and ten from South Asia, including Neera Chandhoke, professor of political science, University of Delhi, and author of *State and Civil Society: Explorations in Political Theory*. The forum received its main funding from the Canadian International Development Agency (CIDA), with additional support from the International Development Research Centre (IDRC), the International Centre for Human Rights and Democratic Development, the North-South Institute, and the Canadian Centre for Foreign Policy Development.

The information, materials, resources, proceedings, and, in general, the interest generated from the forums led to the writing of this book, which was made possible by a grant from the Trillium Foundation.

# Acknowledgements

With the passing of the Cold War "civil society" has been much-discussed, preoccupying those who—not subscribing to any fuzzyminded End of History thinking—would ask "what next?" How to navigate the changing terrain on which government, the market, and voluntary organizations occupy shifting positions? How are those involved in age-old struggles for social justice and equality to make sense of the sudden reappearance of a notion that had long languished in the mists of political theory, only to emerge as a fashionable topic echoing around conference halls from Vancouver to Karachi?

This book had its origins in one such meeting, a 1997 conference organized by the South Asia Partnership. Linda Moffat of SAP-Canada asked me to write a short book that would elaborate on some of the themes that emerged at that forum. She was the moving force behind this book, patiently encouraging me to keep stabbing away at a task that one of her colleagues described as "like trying to pin multi-coloured jelly to a wall." I am indebted to Linda for her cheerful support when I was trying to make sense of it all. Thanks also to Faris Ahmed, Jonathan Barker, Paul Eprile, David Peerla, Mohammad Qadeer, Ian Smillie, Gauri Sreenivasan, Aparna Sundar, Brian Tomlinson, and Alison Van Rooy for useful comment, criticisms, and additions to my bulging civil society files. Jackie Davies brought her sharp, critical thinker's eye to a second draft. And as usual that intrepid editor Robert Clarke made sense of it all, bringing whatever consistency and clarity the jelly's present form takes.

J.S.
Kingston, Ontario

# 1

# Introduction: **Unpacking the Conceptual Ragbag**

> Those who tout it as the silver bullet both to
> "open" repressive societies and to guarantee
> or deepen democratic liberties and curb state
> power move with feline grace between using
> civil society as a descriptive term and as a pre-
> scriptive one.
>
> **David Rieff,** *The Nation*, 1999

Each year since 1990 the United Nations Development
Programme has issued a tidy, accessible, large-format book
packed with statistics and current analysis. Added up, the details are meant to provide the latest sum total of human economic and social progress. The *Human Development Report*
might feature a quote from Gandhi: "The earth provides
enough to satisfy every man's need but not every man's greed."
Or it might show, in a revealing graph, that although South
Asian women made progress in school enrolment between
1970 and 1992, in Bangladesh the average wage of women is
still barely 40 per cent of the amount paid to men. This is a
world in which more than a billion people cannot meet their
basic needs, while (according to one writer) "other consumers—including me and most likely you and the societies in
which we live—are consuming in ways that cannot long be

sustained environmentally or socially and that are quite often inimical to our own well-being."[1]

Each year too, as Canada once again comes out on top of the UN's human development index—a measure that seeks "to capture as many aspects of human development as possible in one simple composite index and to produce a ranking of human development achievements"[2]—the response has been predictable. Like a hometown fan at a hockey game, the prime minister renews a ritual chant. "We're Number One!" The press corps duly records the details of our position of pride.

In a country like Nepal, the reaction may be more muted. Canada is a rich country, Nepal poor. On the UN list Nepal is nestled alongside Yemen and Madagascar, at number 152.

Which does not mean that there are not lots of rich people in the Himalayan kingdom and that poverty is not a problem in Toronto or Tuktoyaktuk. What it does mean is that poverty is a Great Divide, a continuing challenge to a world that spends more on playing golf than on social programs for children, a world in which Europe and the United States spend more on pet food than on the additional funds needed to provide basic health and nutrition throughout the South. The Canadian prime minister, a keen golfer, did not address the 1998 *Human Development Report*'s finding that Canada had slipped to tenth place in that year's new human poverty index, which measured illiteracy, poverty, social exclusion, and unemployment.

That massive poverty exists in a world of unprecedented wealth is no longer a matter of great debate, if it ever was. During the second half of the twentieth century, with the old colonial systems collapsed or overturned, study after study documented the dismal realities and grim prospects for "development" of what would become known as the "majority world." Theorist after theorist presented neat, and sometimes not so neat, solutions for tackling the Great Divide and solving the problems of "underdevelopment." There would be stages of growth, takeoff points, partners in development. In Canada and elsewhere, as governments sent only an irregular dribble of funds and resources in the direction of foreign aid, other institutional forces, large and small, outside government but often connected with it, had to attempt to fill the breach—a case, as we will see, of civil society to the rescue, or at least to the attempted rescue.

As a result the past three to four decades, in both the rich and poor worlds, have seen an explosion in the growth of non-governmental organizations (NGOs), so much so that the phenomenon has been called an "associational revolution." The business of development—the "development enterprise," as I call it—became the preoccupation of a host of these NGOs, and international development became a growth industry. Over two hundred Canadian development NGOs have sprung up along the way. Similarly, in recent years across the South thousands of citizens' groups have emerged, aimed at everything from digging wells to promoting human rights. The World Bank reckons that a 1993 estimate of $5.7 billion in aid going to NGOs undervalued the total by as much as $3 billion.[3] One widely cited estimate claims that there are now some 35,000 NGOs in the South, with 12,000 irrigation co-operatives in South Asia alone. This figure would seem to be low, judging by a statement made by a participant at a 1997 NGO meeting in Nepal who said that Nepal alone had as many as 22,000 NGOs.[4]

In Canada the list of NGOs ranges from large, prominent organizations such as Oxfam to smaller, lesser-knowns such as Horizons of Friendship, based in Cobourg, Ontario. Most if not all of these NGOs receive support from the state, which has, through the Canadian International Development Agency (CIDA), provided funds to a greater or lesser degree to back their work. They are also by definition working outside of the state, perhaps parallel to it, sometimes in opposition to it. Internationally minded NGOs from Oxfam to Amnesty International are only a small part of Canada's non-governmental sector, which includes everything from wilderness preservers to the gun lobby, from anti-poverty groups to service clubs.

All of these NGOs, in Canada and abroad, are part of this thing called "civil society," which, just like this thing called love, can mean many different things to many different people and can operate on highly variable levels of passion and compassion. As a term and concept, civil society has been around for centuries, but it has been revitalized, almost reborn, in recent years. Long familiar to political theorists and academics in sundry subspecialties, the notion of civil society has recently seeped into mainstream political vocabulary. Perhaps it is an idea whose time has come. A search of a leading university's computerized catalogue under "subject" brings up sixty-five entries for "civil society." Only two predate 1990. There is now such a thing as a "civil society manager"—or at least Harvard University has a program to certify people looking to engage in such a role (whatever it is). From the left, gadfly author Jeremy Rifkin holds up a similar term—the "third sector"—as a solution to the vexing problems raised in his 1995 book *The End of Work*. From the right, *The Economist* celebrates civil society in the form of NGOs as a fresh alternative to inefficient government structures in the South. These days, it seems, much is expected of civil society in our efforts to deal with poverty and social exclusion, to promote democracy and human rights.

In essence civil society involves the **activity of citizens in free association who lack the authority of the state**, although the groupings or organizations may have gained access to state resources (and thereby bargained away some of their autonomy). **Such activities are motivated by objectives other than profit-making**, although citizens may undertake income-generating activity as a means of furthering their objectives.

Still, many non-specialists may respond to the term's use by thinking that it must surely have something to do with polite behaviour, with a society in which people trust each other and co-operate in the little transactions of everyday life. Of course, the behaviour we expect from each other varies from place to place and from person to person. It is culturally defined. Getting onto a crowded bus is different in Sri Lanka than it is in Canada. So too it is with the notion of civil society.

Even among the cognoscenti who use the term, civil society can carry a range of meanings. For a young staff person at a Nepalese (or Peruvian or Tanzanian) organization dedicated to improving literacy among women (or organizing farmers or providing micro-credit), it may be a convenient phrase to use in preparing a funding proposal for a Danish (or Canadian or UN) agency. For a *Globe and Mail* writer probing civility, ethics, and values, it means chasing a quote from a Canadian pollster who claims that "there's the sense that the whole moral fibre of society has declined" and citing a U.S. report (*A Call to Civil Society*) urging tougher divorce laws and an end to lotteries.[5] For Indian political theorist Neera Chandhoke, civil society has become "a conceptual ragbag." Chandhoke was the keynote speaker at a series of 1997 conferences organized by the South Asia Partnership (SAP), an alliance of six voluntary development organizations in Canada and South Asia. The conference was titled, with appropriate ambivalence, "Strengthening Civil Society: Progressive Strategy or Smokescreen?"

Civil society hints at voluntarism, charity, community organizing, grassroots activity. It means advocacy groups, representation, citizen engagement, and service delivery. In

Canada civil society groups include not only NGOs like Oxfam, CUSO, and CARE but also the venerable VON (Victorian Order of Nurses) and the 1970s-born lobby group Business Council on National Issues (BCNI), with its agenda of deficit-cutting, social-program slashing, and privatization.* The term, capable of spreading its wings fully wide, can take in the organized labour movement and the organized corporate elite. Organizations as diverse as the World Bank and a peace research institute based in Krgyzstan have come to be deliberating on the meaning of civil society—or perhaps not so much deliberating on it as tossing the concept into the ragbag. In his preface to a 1997 volume on the UN's recent spate of global conferences, for instance, Secretary-General Kofi Annan emphasizes the indispensable role of "women's groups, academics, business people, trade unions *and other members of civil society*."[6]

Civil society is often defined by what it is *not*. When it is understood as formal and informal organizations that are neither part of the state nor part of the market, the concept can cover a tremendous range of groups. Roy Trivedy and Jagabandhu Acharya wonder about a place occupied by such a diversity of social forces:

> By definition civil society consists of a variety of groupings. These include fascists, terrorists, racketeers, criminal elements as well as individuals and groups committed to democracy, and the much fancied neighbourhood organizations. Whatever system of classification one employs however, it would not be difficult to distinguish the

---

* The BCNI is a coalition of corporate leaders formed in 1976 under the leadership of finance capital to promote globalization and the recasting of the Canadian state. It is devoted unequivocally to market principles together with the standard mix of deregulation and privatization that has come to characterize the politics of neo-liberalism.

poor, marginalized sections of society from the richer sections. Do the former have the same interests as the latter?[7]

According to Canada's Business Council on National Issues, its members are chosen "for their public spiritedness and commitment to the betterment of public policies."[8] This sounds benign indeed, much like a phrase from a funding proposal describing the volunteer board of an NGO promoting curbs on pesticide use in Pakistan. In her attempt to understand the real meaning of civil society, Oxfam-America staffer Laura Roper Renshaw raises an important question: "If civil society is supposedly distinct from the apparatus of the state, how do you classify the so-called NGOS that are made up of the same elements that control the economy and/or government?"[9]

In the Third World the term, as we shall see, includes the Sarvodaya Shramadama Movement in Sri Lanka. This "people's movement" emphasizing community self-help began modestly enough, then grew into the country's largest NGO and eventually found itself caught in a tangle of political and organizational problems. The term also covers India's Narmada Bachao Andolan, an organization of tribal peoples who came together to protect their sacred Narmada River from the dam-building onslaught of powerful forces from both inside and outside the country. This is civil society from the ground up. Small, local groups of people who were previously the objects of development—or displacement (they have too often been one and the same)—have emerged to challenge the idea of development from above.

In Southern cities where the state itself has not, for whatever reasons, responded to serious problems of housing, sanitation, transportation, education, and health services, civil society groups have helped to pick up the slack. As researcher Patricia McCarney points out, some urban areas now have "organizations for squatter communities, tenants' associations, savings and credit associations, area development committees, security committees, women's associations, and even independent research and management advisory bodies."[10] These kinds of local, grassroots organizations have the potential of playing a key role in the political future—the governance—of Third World communities.

That use of the term civil society differs from conventional Western views of voluntary, mutual-aid organizations providing services and interest groups competing to get their positions across in the public arena. Civil society groups may do those things but, according to writer Jenny Pearce, an "authentic" civil society—and this is the idealized form that is usually assumed in many NGO discussions—"must involve the poor and the weak gaining real and meaningful rights as citizens, genuinely enfranchised and able to build organizations to defend their interests. It is about the rights of individuals to associate voluntarily. Constructing civil society cannot be essentially about building up intermediary development organizations to represent the 'poor': it must be about empowering the poor and enabling them to fight for their own rights as citizens."[11]

● ● ●

In 1997 Lewis Perinbam told a group of international development workers meeting in Calgary that non-governmental organizations are a vital form of civil society. He quoted Alexis de Tocqueville, the French aristocrat who theorized about nineteenth-century democracy, to the effect that "The health of a democratic society may be measured by the quality of the functions performed by its private citizens." Perinbam described civil society and NGOs as "the wellsprings of an open democracy." He said, *"Most importantly, they have facilitated and directed peoples' participation which has gathered momentum as a potent force in national and international arenas."* And, he added, with a touch of dramatic licence, *"For the first time in history 'people power' is a factor to be reckoned with by governments."*[12]

Perinbam, a long-time advocate of volunteer citizen action, was a founder of CUSO, one of Canada's oldest and best-known NGOs. He went on to become a key promoter (and funder) of NGOs within the Canadian International Development Agency. As much as any other Canadian, Perinbam has for nearly fifty years been at the centre of Canadian NGO efforts aimed at dealing with the South's persistent poverty. "At its best," he told his Calgary audience, this has been "a story of compassion and concern." But, he cautioned, "The aid era has created a new colonialism based on donors and recipients. . . . International development has become an industry."

A compassionate industry? An industry whose product is compassion? Whereas early efforts at international development hinged largely on megaprojects—and in the case of Canadian aid meant large dams—today's emphasis is just as likely to be on "capacity building," enabling groups in Southern civil society to organize themselves, speak for themselves. Perinbam's vocabulary of "private citizens" and "peoples' participation" has become pervasive. In Canada, where a fashionable neo-liberal ideology has meant a return to laissez-faire, government often promotes the idea that "the community" should take upon itself the tasks of providing services once delivered by the welfare state. In the South, neo-liberalism has meant the application of structural adjustment medicine that usually leaves the poor in worse shape than ever. Recently, financial institutions like the World Bank, which have been prescribing massive doses of structural adjustment, are also recommending that it be accompanied by a good, solid measure of civil society.

The international aid system—the development enterprise—has often been buffeted by shifting winds, as trends come and go. Long before structural adjustment there were stages of growth, accompanied by technical assistance for industrialization. There were Green Revolutions, basic needs, women and development, "sustainable development," and human resource development. In the early 1990s the high tide of environmentalism crested. The Earth Summit held in Rio de Janeiro in 1992 was a heady marketplace of ideas, intentions, and resolutions.* Lewis Perinbam reported that Sylvia Ostry, a high-profile Canadian policy entrepreneur, had referred to the Rio Summit as "a watershed event for non-governmental organizations," which were emerging as "main actors" in the age of globalization.[13]

As Rio faded from the public memory, in country after country advocates of laissez-faire continued to occupy the ideological high ground. At the same time, the end of authoritarian state socialism and the command economies of Eastern Europe gave new impetus to questions about the role of the state in economic development. Donor agencies were increasingly emphasizing the importance of strengthening the "civil society" that was seen to have played a critical role in

---

* The Canadian government signed a much-vaunted biodiversity treaty and recommitted itself to applying 0.7 per cent of its Gross National Product to foreign aid. Within months, however, Canada's aid budget was subjected to the first of a series of devastating cuts, while the biodiversity treaty that emerged at Rio was, in the words of London's *Financial Times*, all about "how living organisms could be commercially exploited and who should have the patent rights." Quoted in Tom Athanasiou, *Divided Planet: The Ecology of Rich and Poor* (Boston: Little, Brown, 1996), p. 205.

transforming the Soviet bloc.

It was against this background that the civil society trend hit the development enterprise (as well as the Canadian welfare state). As policy forums and donor documents began to define, examine, and apply civil society as an organizing concept, cynics responded by labelling the discovery of civil society as the latest "flavour of the month." Indeed, in the world of the development enterprise, civil society has become, rightly or wrongly, shorthand for NGOs. But NGO-watcher Alan Fowler has described attempts to get a grip on civil society as "like trying to pin multi-coloured jelly to a wall; difficult to see in its totality because we are all made colour blind by our own ways of looking at the world, while its fluid composition makes the concept hard to grasp."[14]

An establishment view of civil society comes from the United States Agency for International Development. USAID argues that all countries, and especially those emerging from authoritarian rule, need organizations that are autonomous from government, and that civil society is crucial in promoting the accountability of the state. Americans have a long tradition of suspicion when it comes to the state. As a society racked by violence and fear, the United States has recently become preoccupied with what many regard as a decline in civic participation. Add to these factors U.S. geopolitical concerns, the imperatives of a post-Cold War world, and the Clinton White House's intellectual flirtation with communitarianism, and it is hardly surprising that the country's official aid agency should respond.

USAID has spent a lot of money on civil society programming. The emphasis is on institutions that will pressure and influence government, so that there is much talk about "governance" (but little mention of, say, "mobilization"). USAID has also invested significant intellectual capital in the subject, helping to shape thinking at the influential Development Assistance Committee of the Organization for Economic Co-operation and Development (OECD). USAID documents express a concern for "the democracy sector," concentrating on what the agency now calls "civic advocacy organizations" (CAOs), having adopted this term over its earlier "civil society organizations." USAID is careful to differentiate such groups from more generic "NGOs" that provide humanitarian relief or promote economic and social development activities. USAID defines civic advocacy organizations as non-state groups engaged in lobbying government or, in official parlance, "groups that engage in or have the potential for championing, adoption and consolidation of democratic governance reforms." Under this broad umbrella is crowded an uneasy collection of organizations—labour federations, policy think-tanks, business and professional associations, human rights and pro-democracy groups, environmental groups, "and the like."[15]

This view of civil society brings to mind the old stages of growth theory of economic development. In the 1950s and 1960s, when donors were obsessed with building dams, the dominant idea was that the postcolonial world should proceed with large-scale industrial developments, following the "development" path pounded down so well by former colonial powers. Applied to civil society and democracy, the urge to mimic the modernity of the West ignores the democratic forms indigenous to many premodern and preliberal societies. The export version of civil society used by USAID reflects a pluralistic, technical view of politics, traditional American liberalism as it is played out inside Washington's beltway and at sundry state legislatures: interest groups, policy briefs, lobbying . . . and the like. For political scientist Benjamin Barber, the idea of the American version of democracy as export commodity is absurd: "Fed Ex the Federalist Papers to Belorussia; send a multiparty system to Nigeria by parcel post; e-mail the Chinese the Bill of Rights. . . . Not quite. Democracies are built slowly, culture by culture, each with its own strengths and needs, over centuries."[16]

In a recommendation that will sound familiar to Canadian psychiatric self-help groups and literacy programs reeling from state cutbacks, USAID advises Southern civil society organizations to wean themselves from traditional sources of funds (such as grants from "national and international donors"):

> It is particularly important to develop organizational skills in raising funds from more diverse domestic sources (such as membership fees, corporate giving, and sales of goods and services). Skills in policy and institutional analysis are of paramount importance. To arrive at a cogent and convincing reform agenda, CAOs must undertake the analysis necessary to prepare technically well-grounded proposals for policy and institutional changes they advocate. . . . Many CAOs lack these skills.[17]

This is politics at a formal, textbook level. It reflects a world view that sees political competition in the same way that classical economists regard the market, a place in which rivalry and choice generate outcomes that benefit all consumers. The "real world" (a construct popular with marketeers) is, unfortunately, a place in which neat models rarely work. USAID is a sophisticated outfit that acknowledges the difficulty of these matters. It recognizes that the transition to democracy in the South is "uneven, messy, and subject to setbacks." At least in this sense, the agency has it right. Democracy—in Canada, the United States, India, Bangladesh, wherever—is an ideal, a route to be taken rather than a destination reached.

Echoing U.S. philosopher John Dewey's description of democracy as a way of life, not a way of government, Douglas Lummis's book *Radical Democracy* describes it not as any particular set of economic or political institutions but as "the name of a political form in which the people have power." In this view, democracy is the goal of government, not a kind of government, "not a historically existing institution but a historical project." As a historical project, democracy moves in fits and starts. Forces with different interests and values come into conflict. It varies from country to country, from time to time. Like civil society, democracy is something everyone apparently favours, but (again, like civil society) it means many different things to many different people. Some equate democracy with the free market. Or voting. Or free elections. For some, democracy equals "development." Others believe that a democracy is a caring society that helps the weak.

For Lummis, civil society can be part of the historical project of democracy: "Civil society provides *space* for public discourse, for the development of public values and public language, for the formation of the public self (the citizen), a space separate from the formal political sphere dominated by state power and political parties that aim to control that power."[18] Lummis quotes Adam Ferguson, a Scots philosopher and eighteenth-century contemporary of famed economist Adam Smith. Ferguson mused that in civil society the citizen has a place to "act in the view of his fellow creatures, to produce his mind in public," and that didn't mean having to become a politician. As Lummis puts it, "Civil society does not demand freedom, but generates it."[19]

• • •

Like "democracy," civil society is, then, a complex term, a concept of inherent paradox. For one thing the organizations of civil society were by definition to be outside the state; yet they often came to depend on the state to help solve the problems they were most concerned with. The state and civil society would form interdependent, though not necessarily equal, units. The Sardinian communist Antonio Gramsci theorized, for instance, that Western Europe's well-developed institutions of civil society (including trade unions) served to act as shock absorbers for the state. Yet despite these complexities and contradictions, as Neera Chandhoke pointed out, civil society "has become a bit of a hurrah!-word. This means it has positive connotations as opposed to a boo!-word which would carry negative connotations. . . . Civil society, a bit like democracy, has become a self-validating flag."[20]

One way of gaining an understanding of civil society is to see the concept not just as a matter of individual citizens or organizations but as a space between official public life (government) and private life (especially the market). "Between the economic structure and the State with its legislation and coercion," wrote Gramsci, "stands civil society."[21]

Extending the metaphor of civil-society-as-place, we can imagine how its borders with the market and the government are blurred. Civil society is a very large space, and it is terrain that is frequently contested. Every group, every NGO, every social movement, every voluntary group—each of them has its own conflicting internal dynamics involving power and authority, means and ends. How does the organization's agenda get shaped? Who shapes it? Does everybody involved—male and female, educated and uneducated, rich and poor, black and white—have an equal say? Who is accountable to whom? These interesting, thorny, and eternal questions are never easy to sort out.

The problem with the blanket use of the term civil society is that it fails to specify the objectives of the activities being undertaken. The goal may include resistance to market forces, as in the case of people organizing workers in a free-trade zone. It may be to oppose the state, as in the case of Poland's famous Solidarity, an independent trade union movement formed in 1980. Civil society may also complement the market and the state by fulfilling needs not met by either, which is the case with many NGOs. Activities undertaken by citizens acting in civil society may prop up the state and maintain the stability so important to market forces. According to a background paper on strengthening civil society issued by the U.K.-based International Non-governmental Organization Training and Research Centre (INTRAC):

> Relationships between civil society and the state are highly complex and operate at multiple levels of engagement. Rather than seeking to identify certain types of organizations which fit a restricted definition of civil society, the task for social analysts is to undertake a much broader organizational mapping and seek to understand the complex way . . . in which groups interact with each other and with the state. . . . Rather than equating civil society with democracy, it is necessary to identify what elements within civil society are likely to promote democracy, and equally, what elements of civil society are likely to resist it.[22]

What is clear is that we can't assume that civil society is an unalloyed force for Good. Indeed, civil society has an organic relationship with society—a relationship mirroring the ethnic, gender, and class fractures that exist within every society.

Many of today's theorists of civil society employ a three-cornered model that posits the state, the market, and civil society as distinct, almost separate, entities. Within this trinity, much is made of a "third sector" of independent associations comprising free citizens contending with state and market. Sometimes this is described as the "voluntary sector," and it includes, foremost among the lot, non-governmental organizations. The emphasis is usually on dynamism and flexibility, factors juxtaposed to rigid, heavy-handed state structures. The invisible hand of market forces is usually neglected, or assumed.

Jessica Mathews, a senior fellow at Washington's Council on Foreign Relations, has pointed to "the rise of global civil society" and the decline in the power of the state. She celebrates this development, placing particular emphasis on NGOs as substitutes for the welfare state in the North and alternatives to state provision in the South: "Internationally, in both the poorest and the richest countries, NGOs, when adequately funded, can outperform government in the delivery of many public services. Their growth, along with that of the other elements of civil society, can strengthen the fabric of the many still-fragile democracies. . . . Nation-states may simply no longer be the natural problem-solving unit."[23]

According to this perspective, a "power shift" is underway, with the state on the wane and civil society on the rise. This power shift includes little consideration of capital, whose increased power has contributed to the relative decline of states. Nor is ideology the main factor: "The most powerful engine of change in the relative decline of states and the rise of nonstate actors is the computer and the telecommunications revolution." Digital technologies "have the potential to divide society along new lines, separating ordinary people from elites with the wealth and education to command technology's power. Those elites are not only the rich but also citizens' groups with transnational interests and identities that frequently have more in common with counterparts in other countries, whether industrialized or developing, than with countrymen."[24]

An important turning point was the Earth Summit of 1992, when NGOs moved out of the hallways, "penetrating deeply into official decision making." Mathews points to NGOs both large and small, from the activist Greenpeace and the huge service-provider CARE to the tiny South Asian irrigation co-operatives, as evidence of the new scope and power of civil society. NGOs can apparently now "push governments around"—as Mathews maintains they did during negotiations over the North American Free Trade Agreement.

Although the unabashed claims it makes on behalf of civil society are perhaps exceptional, this analysis is not atypical of official infatuation with an ostensibly new age of non-state actors. There is, however, a huge problem with this sort of New Age-ism. "Civil society" has become such a catch-all category that it can embrace an incredibly broad and varied range of groups, many of them operating at cross-purposes. What use is theorizing that attempts to explain the workings and goals of a peasant women's self-help organization in Uttar Pradesh and a wilderness conservation group in Canada? The answer can only lie in scrutinizing the motives and priorities of those using the term, taking into account the background of civil society's re-emergence after several decades of languishing in relative obscurity in university libraries and seminar rooms.

What, too, does all the talk of civil society offer to NGOs that seek to address unequal power relations? Certainly, if the remarks by a highly placed Canadian politician are anything to go by, government sees a role for the voluntary sector:

"Government . . . is tapping into the collective wisdom, talents, and strengths that are 'out there' in the realm of civil society and the private sector. . . . NGOs have always served as our collective conscience, and as a vehicle for citizen participation . . . closest to the people. They know what is needed. And they have a credibility that government often lacks."[25]

In some South Asian countries the "associational revolution" of the NGO factor has been particularly intense. The Bangladesh Rural Advancement Committee (BRAC) employs over 12,000 people and has a multi-storey corporate headquarters. Sri Lanka's large Sarvodaya NGO says it has workers in 8,000 villages. NGOs are increasingly popular with government and multilateral donors. They are allegedly "closest to the people" and can claim greater legitimacy than governments. At the same time, NGOs are said to be highly efficient, with BRAC negotiating $50 million aid packages with donor "consortia." NGOs from both North (CARE) and South (BRAC) are increasingly viewed as service delivery vehicles in preference to the state. According to David Hulme and Michael Edwards, "the rise of NGOs is not an accident" but is part of a policy agenda "driven by beliefs organized around the twin poles of neoliberal economics and liberal democratic policies."[26]

Activists and NGOs concerned with participation and empowerment must certainly be aware that much inequality of rank, position, and remuneration exists within NGOs and all the other manifestations of civil society—between women and men, for instance—and that in this they are a mirror of society at large. A key tenet of civil society must be to work to ensure that the voices of those traditionally excluded are heard. This task of empowerment is all about making sure that people who had none get some—and not about entrenching the power of NGOs (however well-intentioned) that are assisting in the process.

This, again, is not an easy task, but it must first of all involve the recognition that any activity that creates a significant and effective space for the excluded is a political activity. The activity can change local power relationships and patterns of distribution and ownership. An irrigation project may be a huge endeavour sponsored by the state and backed by the World Bank. Or it may be undertaken by a grassroots organization in partnership with a small Canadian NGO. In either case, the same questions arise. Whose land gets irrigated? Does the project reinforce or challenge existing patterns of land ownership? Are the poor involved in the planning from the beginning, with grassroots organizations having some control of the project? Or does participation follow the familiar decide-announce-defend model? Does the activity democratize unequal power relations? In short, who pays? Who profits?

These questions are critical, and eternal. Sometimes they concern NGOs from megamillion-dollar multinational aid agencies like CARE to small organizations like CoDevelopment Canada or the Mennonite Central Committee. Often they do not. The Canadian Council for International Co-operation (the umbrella organization representing development NGOs) has taken the position that successfully tackling the mammoth problem of global poverty depends on citizens participating in a redefinition of the political process: "NGOs can promote citizen participation by setting an example. . . . Northern NGOs face the challenge of developing equitable relationships with the Southern groups they support. This means working together to determine how and where money will be invested. It also means replacing hierarchical power structures with egalitarian ways of making decisions."[27]

• • •

Introducing his 1990 Gunnar Myrdal lecture, U.S. political theorist Michael Walzer noted that he had "no hope" of theoretical simplicity in applying himself to his subject, "The Idea of Civil Society." Rather, he was setting out to defend a "complex, imprecise," and "uncertain account of society and politics."[28] So it is with discussions of civil society. It would be easy enough to return to the simple (and accurate enough) observation that civil society can mean all things to all people. It would be a straightforward matter to denounce the concept as a stalking horse for neo-liberalism. It might be tempting to see it, as Trivedy and Acharya do, as "projecting an idealized Western model of parliamentary democracy as the historic destiny of humanity—as if equality and human rights prevailed in the developed West!"[29] It could be seen as a theory that fails, as Alan Fowler points out, to "incorporate the reality of non-organic states." Fowler warns, "Informal relations, associations and organizations which people value—often forming an important element in survival strategies of people who are poor—are either ignored, treated as 'pre-civic,' or viewed as sources of anti-social, anti-modern behaviour which need to be eradicated. Yet, across the world, informalism based on trust is a significant factor in maintaining social stability as well as reducing the cost of economic transactions."[30]

These caveats have considerable merit. But where do they leave people active in organizations struggling for justice and equality, South and North? For Richard Harmston, executive director of SAP Canada, introducing the proceedings at the 1997 SAP conferences, civil society can either be seen as a fad sweeping through the international development and aid community or as "a profound expression of common people struggling to change their world." It is the second, *engagé* view that animates this book—a view that sees civil society as a potential means to an end rather than an honorific category.

Even if civil society has become fashionable in the international aid system, and if it has been used in vague, unhelpful ways, it remains an important concept in the struggle for global justice. Basic needs, the participation of women in development, environmental sustainability: these once-fashionable imperatives may no longer capture the attention of donors or the media to the extent that they once did, but they continue to reflect fundamental challenges for activists and agencies working globally or locally. Likewise, civil society can help us figure out which side of the fence we are on . . . and who is there with us.

**②**

# The Politics of Helping People:
# Canada and Sri Lanka

> Most men and women have been trapped in
> one or another subordinate relationship, where
> the "civility" they learned was deferential rather
> than independent and active. That is why
> democratic citizenship, socialist production, free
> enterprise, and nationalism were all of them
> liberating projects. But none of them has yet
> produced a general, coherent, or sustainable
> liberation.
>
> Michael Waltzer, 1990

"You pay peanuts and you get monkeys!" declared an angry
picket sign carried by a home-care nurse outside the office of
the Victorian Order of Nurses in Kingston, Ontario. Another
sign said: "RPNs take the cuts, the VON makes the bucks."

In 1998 the Registered Practical Nurses employed by the
VON in Ontario went on strike. The proud VON pin that had
for so long adorned the starched, neatly pressed uniforms of
dedicated home nurses was in danger of being tarnished by
bitter confrontation. A non-profit organization that describes
itself as "a Canadian treasure" found itself immersed in a
decidedly messy conflict. With community-based home-care
services at the top of Canada's health-care agenda, with local

organizations apparently poised to deliver them, the VON—the voluntary sector *par excellence*—was accused of being a stingy zookeeper.

Founded in 1897 to provide nursing care for people in the country's remote districts (or, as writer Sarah Jane Crowe puts it, "to close the gap between home and hospital")[1] the VON evolved into a well-organized charitable group providing nursing services to people who need everything from help with their dentures and feet to palliative care and home nursing after hospitalization. In some regions the VON marshals an army of volunteers who prepare hot meals and deliver them as part of the highly successful Meals-on-Wheels program, so crucial in enabling older people to remain in their own homes. Since the beginning the VON has been for the most part managed and staffed by women.

The VON is run by volunteer boards operating at the national and provincial levels. It identifies itself as a community-based charity dedicated to helping the sick, the bereaved, and the needy. Like many philanthropic initiatives, it has its roots in nineteenth-century, Victorian notions of charity. Canada's famous nursing corps was founded by Lady Ishbel Aberdeen, wife of Canada's then governor-general. She was a forceful and energetic woman who, before coming to Canada, had helped to form the Onward and Upward Society, a Scottish group dedicated to promoting literacy, morality, and domestic skills among female servants. In Canada she teamed up with women active in the Dominion Women's Enfranchisement Association and the National Council of Women to establish, on the occasion of Queen Victoria's 1897 Diamond Jubilee, an organization that would provide health-care services to outlying districts of the country.

The aim was to provide home helpers who would care for the sick and spread up-to-date ideas about health and sanitation, "caring for the sick and suffering in their own homes." Overcoming vigorous opposition from a male medical establishment that was just then consolidating its control over modern health care and centralizing that care in hospitals, the VON sought out people living in poverty who could not afford health care—miners, shantymen, and their families— recognizing local needs and exploring ways of meeting them. It established a national network of small-town cottage hospitals that supplemented the services of its successful visiting nurses. It would soon become the only organization in the country providing formal training in public health. From the earliest days it augmented its private fundraising among the well-to-do with grants from various levels of government and important contracts with the Metropolitan Life Insurance Company to provide visiting care to policyholders.

Later on the consolidation of the postwar welfare state and the growth of hospital-based health care changed the VON's position. A principal source of revenue became home-care contracting for provincial governments, although the organization continued to offer a wide range of community services at a nominal charge, if not free. It placed particular emphasis on day programs and support services for old people as well as doing support and respite work on behalf of the increasing number of women who had paid jobs but were still expected to care for aging relatives. The VON did innovative work in developing well-baby programs and nurse-practitioner services aimed at relieving pressure on primary care physicians in family practice. The organization quickly became a major employer of nurses and nursing assistants, most of them women. As welfare-state industries like education and health care became unionized, so too did many of the VON's employees.

By the latter part of the twentieth century the organization was clearly no longer a paternalistic charity holdover from the late Victorian era. The VON had gradually become influenced by what it now describes as "new ideas about the nature of health." The conviction that health care should not be the only—or even the primary—focus in dealing with health matters came to the fore. VON Chief Executive Officer Donna Roe would argue that the "VON's strong grassroots base can be very effective in dealing with the problems of poverty, poor nutrition and unemployment—the determinants of health." The VON, as do so many other non-profit organizations, often frames this health promotion approach in the vocabulary of community development: "Lasting change can only be brought about by empowerment of communities to help themselves."[2]

At the same time that it was recognizing the importance of empowering poor people as a way of dealing with the causes of illness and the promotion of health, the VON felt the ground shifting beneath its feet. Governments began to cut spending on health care and forced the organization to compete with well-capitalized private-sector operators. The state was responding with passivity to the poverty and nutrition problems that contribute so significantly to ill health among the poor.

Cathy Bonnah, a VON health promotion worker, saw what was happening as "a strong backlash" against the welfare state. The idea was, she said, that "if individuals had problems, it was their own fault," and they then had the responsibility of picking themselves up "by the bootstraps." The view that was increasingly underpinning both government policy and the social attitudes of some Canadians, Bonnah said, was "a throwback to a mythical past where friends and family looked after each other, and there was no need for organized assistance."[3] By the time of the 1998 Kingston strike (one of a spate of labour conflicts that hit the organization that year), Ivan Ip, executive director of the Eastern Lake Ontario branch of the

VON, was talking about market competition and the need to revamp the organization's internal cost structure.

Government-mandated competition from private health-care corporations had put the voluntary sector and nurses on the defensive. Both sides in the dispute agreed that their problems related directly to the government's decision to open community nursing up to for-profit health-care companies. Historically, most home nursing services in Kingston had been provided by the VON and the Public Health Unit, with the costs covered by the provincial government. This changed after the election, in 1995, of a provincial government with a market-driven agenda. Home care was to be tendered, just like road paving contracts, and budgets capped. Henceforth, home nursing contracts would be given to the voluntary organization or business that made the best offer, and a significant component in this decision would be the lowest cost. Since wages, salaries, benefits, and transportation make up 94 per cent of the VON's visiting-nurse program's costs, free-market competition inevitably meant cutting the wages and eroding the working conditions of visiting nurses. Even before the Kingston strike, registered practical nurses had lost paid breaks, uniform allowances, agreed to a 1 per cent wage reduction, and given up two paid holidays, bereavement leave for part-time nurses, and shift premiums. The nurses had also agreed to a two-year wage freeze.

Visiting nurses had traditionally earned less than their hospital counterparts, though the VON has tried to pay fair wages. At the time of the strike, Registered Practical Nurses at Kingston General Hospital made a top wage of $18.77 an hour. Top wage at the VON was $17.55, while Comcare, the VON's major local competitor, was paying a top wage of $13.83. (Six months before the VON strike, home-care nurses staged a bitter strike at Comcare, a company controlled in part by the Toronto-Dominion Bank.) As a result of the strike the nurses, fearing the prospect of working for a private-care delivery outfit or losing their jobs altogether, made further concessions.

With state policy slowly edging public health care into another corner of the marketplace, a respected community-based agency and its employees were caught in the squeeze.

"The VON is going through great turmoil in terms of how to identify ourselves," says Bill Gekoski, a twenty-year VON volunteer and former president of the organization in Ontario. Gekoski is proud of the VON and its culture of care. He originally got involved in a program that provided foot care, giving old people increased mobility. He points to the non-profit organization's strong links with other community groups, particularly the local service club that has been helping the VON since 1934. The Kinsmen Club gave them their first building for a dollar and contributed $150,000 when the nursing service moved into new premises.

The VON, however, is not just a popular charity that relies on the good will of the public. "Government-funded visiting nursing is the huge bulk of what we do," Gekoski says. "We have people who feel we should get out of visiting nursing, that if the government isn't prepared to pay reasonable salaries to our nurses, we shouldn't be complicit in what they are doing. We also have people who say we should treat visiting nursing simply as a cost centre, running it for a profit that we can turn back into other programs."[4]

The VON is neither a government agency nor a business, so it qualifies as part of civil society. Its origins were and its motivations are charitable, not-for-profit. It is run by a volunteer board and uses volunteers to provide some of its services. But at the same time it is a major employer. It has become dependent on government and as a result has been subjected to "great turmoil" as government begins to favour the economic structures of the market. As a result, some people within the organization want it to behave more and more like a private business. The VON is caught in the political and economic crosscurrents of society at large.

What to do? Along with its other programs, the VON has been providing home-care services while paying decent wages to the women who furnish those services, only to face mandated competition from low-wage operators. In an age when competition is apparently the only solution on offer—whatever the problem—the invisible hand of the market becomes the preferred tool of the highly visible hand of the state. Where does this leave the Third Hand—the third sector, the community, NGOs, citizen's groups—civil society?

• • •

Civil society as a concept emerged with the eighteenth-century Scottish enlightenment and two Adams born in 1723: Adam Smith (capitalism's most famous theorist); and Adam Ferguson, a Presbyterian minister. Ferguson's *Essay on the History of Civil Society* (1767) and Smith's *An Inquiry into the Nature and Causes of the Wealth of Nations* (1776) soon became standard texts. Less well-known is an address Ferguson made on behalf of the English army sent to put down the Scottish Jacobite rebellion.

Ferguson's patroness, the Duchess Dowager of Athole, was a member of a prominent pro-English family of Scottish aristocrats. Her son became a full colonel of the Highland Black Watch Regiment at the tender age of twenty-two.

Anxious to provide her young son with a companion who would "exercise a wholesome influence," the Duchess had Ferguson appointed deputy-chaplain of the regiment, even though he had not been ordained as a Presbyterian minister. Shortly before the battle of Culloden in 1746 Ferguson found himself delivering a sermon, in Gaelic, to the men of the regiment, urging them to remain steadfast in their service to King George II. According to a biographer, Ferguson's speech to the men, whose loyalty the Crown doubted, was brimming with "patriotic fervour and sharp denunications" of the Scottish rebels.[5]

The English victory at Culloden set the stage for agricultural enclosure and the clearances of common lands. Exiles from these events would be scattered throughout the world to various Outposts of Empire. One of those places was Ceylon, where the British colonial administration was putting its stamp on traditional society with measures that included the introduction of missionary societies—what might now be called church-based NGOs. But, as with the Scottish Highlands and their clan structure before they were made safe for an export-oriented trade and industry, Ceylon already had its own forms of "civil society." Part of daily life for centuries, these practices included informal arrangements and organizations concerned with agriculture, religion, and the life of the community in general, from burial societies to informal mutual assistance initiatives. These indigenous institutions were eroded as the colonial administration (and later the postcolonial state) took over their functions. During the twentieth century the growth of the formal cash economy led to shortages of money, prompting village organizations to adopt more formal structures. Specific funeral assistance and mutual aid societies emerged. Part of the nationalist response to colonialism was the growth of

Buddhist, Hindu, and Muslim institutions promoting educa-tion and cultural life. The arrival of the Young Men's Christian Association in 1882 was followed fifteen years later by the establishment of the Young Men's Buddhist Association. By 1906 a disciplined and effective strike of Colombo carters caught the colonial authorities by surprise, prompting Governor Henry Blake to remark: "That 5000 carters should abandon their work at a word shows a power of organization and combination that cannot be ignored in considering the possibilities of the future."[6]

Independence for Ceylon, in 1948, came not as part of a mass popular struggle but as part of a high-level accommoda-tion. (One academic wag noted that although D.S. Senanayake, the first leader of independent Ceylon, was invari-ably described as the Architect of Ceylon's Freedom, "The structure raised by the British remained intact.")[7] The post-colonial settlement contained ethnic tensions for a time. Sri Lanka (the country's name was changed in 1972) boasted a well-developed welfare state and a strong electoral system. Government, both the colonial authority and successor regimes, took an active role in managing the co-operative soci-eties, rural development initiatives, and credit institutions that grew up alongside independent organizations. Relative pros-perity was accompanied by public provision of education, health, housing, and other services, with 40 to 50 per cent of public expenditures in the 1950s and 1960s being invested in the social-welfare system.[8]

Few of the major development NGOs that were sprouting up throughout the South with the support of external donors took root in Sri Lanka. One exception was the Sarvodaya Shramadama Movement, founded in 1956 by a charismatic schoolteacher, A.T. Ariyaratne. The word "Sarvodaya," borrowed from Gandhi, alluded to a social order different from capitalist and socialist models. Calling itself "a people's movement," Sarvodaya rejects the "Western model of development" as unbalanced because it fails to emphasize community self-help. It says that model concentrates instead on:

> the exploitation of scarce resources to the maximum, apply-
> ing profit-maximizing technologies to the fullest, fuelling
> human greed through a variety of commercial means and
> catering to the utmost gratification of the five senses. This
> has brought affluence to a small section of the world's pop-
> ulation mostly living in the industrialized countries, and
> poverty and powerlessness to the vast majority of people in
> the rest of the world. Large development projects whose
> ultimate result is to make the rich richer and the poor
> poorer have received huge financial resources by way of
> grants and loans from aid donors.[9]

Starting with the growth of village-based Shramadama Camps, the organization used local self-help initiatives as a spring-board for wider programs emphasizing popular participation in the construction of sustainable, "no-poverty/no-affluence" structures at the local level. These, it was hoped, would trans-form society in its image. Well ahead of its time in questioning conventional models of growth and favouring grassroots par-ticipation, Sarvodaya managed to spread its message through-out Sri Lanka. The movement stated that 8,000 villages have "had the Shramadama experience" and that 2,000 villages had registered societies with elected officeholders.[10] By the 1990s Sarvodaya was Sri Lanka's largest NGO, with its own printing press and office building. It had become a favourite of Northern donor agencies anxious to support its vision of development. Like Canada's VON, it had grown like Topsy. Although some critics would say its institutional strength makes it a doubtful candidate for the civil society sphere, its occupation of the non-state, non-profit space does bring it under the civil society umbrella. While the VON calls itself a "national treasure," Sarvodaya quotes Japan's Niwano Peace Foundation, which describes the Sri Lankan organization as "the world's largest citizen-led movement conducted by an NGO."[11]

By 1991 Sarvodaya found itself tangled in controversy, under attack from the government and involved in bickering with its international funders. The president of Sri Lanka launched a commission of inquiry to investigate alleged malpractice among NGOs, with Sarvodaya as the focal point of the probe. The government-controlled *Sunday Observer* carried the headline "Sarvodaya goes from humble village to big-time commercial loan shark." A press campaign accused Ariyaratne of being a billionaire and Sarvodaya of selling children abroad while pouring millions "into black holes."

Meanwhile a consortium of international donor agencies, including Sarvodaya's largest and most important sponsor (NOVIB of the Netherlands) and the Canadian International Development Agency, began to monitor its operations more closely, insisting on more comprehensive financial and administrative control systems. Sarvodaya complained that the donors that had once made it the NGO of choice in the country and one of the most famous in the South were being heavy-handed and pushy. "Hordes of evaluators, monitors, experts and consultants had a field day in Sarvodaya," wrote Jehan Perera, director of the Sarvodaya Legal Service. "Some of them were strangers to people's participatory development movements. . . . We were treated as a subcontractor, not a partner. The natural expansion of the Movement from village to village was interrupted."[12] A Canadian consultant involved with the creation of the Sarvodaya donor consortium had a different analysis of the organization's local undertakings:

> Much of the activity was ephemeral, based on one-off work camps and group meetings to discuss Sarvodaya's ideals of sharing, peace, and co-operative village life. The consortium provided money to consolidate these activities in the 2000 most active villages, and to establish concrete health, nutrition and income-generating activities. More concerned about the spread of its message than specific development efforts, however, Sarvodaya kept growing, even as donor money began to flag. Failing to receive the kind of satisfaction it expected, the consortium finally placed conditions on its support, conditions that Sarvodaya either would not or could not accept.[13]

Just exactly what happened to this seemingly laudable grass-roots venture is not easy to discern. But a combination of factors contributed to the challenges that Sarvodaya faced. Some were of its own making, others beyond its control.

During the immediate postcolonial period Sri Lanka, or Ceylon as it was still called, had money to spend on public initiatives because of solid earnings from commodity exports. Tea, the country's main agricultural export, fetched 2.61 rupees per pound in 1954. But over time, and especially when other producers, particularly in Kenya, Malawi, and Uganda, got in on the action, the price of tea fell. By 1969 tea was earning 1.53 rupees per pound. With the decline in export earnings the government experienced dramatic balance of payments problems, running in the red, on average, to $60 million annually between 1966 and 1975. By 1975 Sri Lanka had a debt of a billion dollars, and debt service charges were eating up 20 per cent of its annual foreign exchange earnings.[14] That was a year after the United Nations—against the wishes of the United

States, the United Kingdom, and Germany—proclaimed the New International Economic Order, calling for (among other things) fair commodity prices. Along with many other Third World countries, Sri Lanka saw its external debt skyrocket during the 1970s, rising from 2.8 million rupees in 1971 to 13.3 million rupees in 1977.[15]

With the end of the long postwar boom and an economy increasingly hobbled by debt, Sri Lanka entered a period of low growth. The country experienced significant increases in social inequality. In 1970-77, the top 10 per cent of income earners accounted for 30 per cent of the total income. By 1985 they accounted for 49 per cent. By contrast the share of the bottom 40 per cent declined from 15 per cent to 7 per cent in the same period.[16] By 1986-87 fully 28 per cent of households were not getting enough to eat, having fallen below the poverty line defined by the UN's World Health Organization and Food and Agriculture Organization calorie allowance.[17] By this time economic deterioration was accompanied by internal political strife as an uprising by youth in the south in the early 1970s was followed by an armed secessionist insurrection by Tamils in the North. The central government responded in kind. After its election victory in 1977 the rightist United National Party embarked on a neo-liberal path that combined laissez-faire economics with a highly authoritarian political stance. General elections were postponed, and violence became endemic. At least six Sarvodaya workers—committed to non-violence—were murdered in the late 1980s.

During that time of crisis Sarvodaya's institutional growth took off. In general the erosion of the welfare state and dramatic increases in poverty provided fertile ground for the nurturing of NGOs. Sarvodaya was already well-known in international circles, receiving project funding from a wide range of multilateral and bilateral government sources as well as Northern NGOs. Foreign funders at the more enlightened end of the donor spectrum were attracted to its message of self-reliance and participatory development, with the Dutch agency NOVIB playing the lead role in providing program funding for the organization in the mid-1980s.[18]

By the 1990s it was one of the largest NGOs in Asia, as much Institution as Movement. It delivered training programs, undertook job-creation initiatives, and sponsored savings organizations. In 1977 A.T. Ariyaratne had said that he expected Sarvodaya to be financially self-sufficient by 1985.[19] The opposite happened. Between 1986 and 1994 it received over $20 million from its donor consortium. But even before the consortium was established Sarvodaya had felt the effects of dependence on external sources when in 1983 NOVIB temporarily withdrew all aid because it believed Sarvodaya had not been vigorous enough in criticizing Tamil massacres. By the early 1990s conflicts with donors had again arisen, with consortium demands for more accountability and tighter management controls provoking angry reactions from the Sri Lankans who were, as they say, "on the ground." While admitting that, like organizations everywhere, there had been waste and misappropriation, Sarvodaya called the donor pressure bureaucratic and rigid, putting the blame for the problems on a "fundamental clash of cultures." It was, Perera stated, "a classic example of an uneven confrontation between the dominant materialistic value-system of the 'northern' development paradigm and the humanistic and holistic approach to development in the South." According to Perera, "The donors even went to the extent of imposing 'sanctions' on Sarvodaya by adducing reasons such as our inability to meet their 'expectations.' Ironically, this is the same type of language used by the IMF

[International Monetary Fund] in dealing with the governments of developing countries."[20]

While confronting its strained relationships with its donors, Sarvodaya also had to face a major confrontation with the Sri Lanka government in the form of the aggressive commission of inquiry into NGOs. Launched by UNP president Ranasinghe Premadasa in 1991, the inquiry was by most accounts aimed at destabilizing Sarvodaya, the largest and best-known NGO in the country. The police arrested and interrogated Sarvodaya staff. Property was seized and accusations of loansharking and baby-selling were complemented by charges of noise and air pollution from a government that did not generally strong-arm industrial polluters or invest much energy in environmental regulation.

The Premadasa regime was led by a cagey, egotistical politician who viewed NGOs as a political force. Sarvodaya was led by a well-known public figure himself not known for retreating from the public spotlight. Both of the leaders were capable of drawing large crowds out to public rallies. In a country both torn by political violence and experiencing a dramatic growth in poverty and inequality, it is not surprising that an organization preaching non-violence and social justice while organizing on a mass basis would confront official harassment. Ariyaratne had been critical of the UNP government's structural adjustment program, which had generated economic growth but led to mass poverty. By the time the commission reported (without being able to come up with criminal charges against Sarvodaya), President Premadasa had been assassinated on May Day, 1993. The new president, apparently keen to restore more cordial relations with Sarvodaya and NGOs in general, telephoned Ariyaratne within days of assuming office. A measure of stability was restored to Sarvodaya's relations with the government.

According to a Sri Lankan critic of NGOs—a man who regards the elected government as the sole source of authority in the country—the tension between the government and Sarvodaya was not confined to the UNP regime. Ranjith Wanigaratne argued, "Over the years both liberal democratic and radical democratic party governments had sought to weaken the role of Sarvodaya. By 1990, NGO activity in general and Sarvodaya in particular, were seen as a 'thorn in the flesh' of the government." The same observer, in a thinly veiled reference to Sarvodaya, criticized NGOs whose activities involved "transplanted pockets of so-called 'participatory development' maintained by external funds, catering quite often to alien development paradigms, [which] remained aloof from the historically evolved domestic sociocultural base."[21]

Ironically, the vocabulary of "external" notions of development and "alien development paradigms" is almost an exact mirror of Sarvodaya's attack on foreign donors. The organization had accused them of imposing "northern development paradigms" on its Shramadama villages and other Sri Lankan programs.

The dilemmas faced by Sarvodaya, though extreme, typify those faced by NGOs that crowd under the civil society umbrella. An organization dedicated to social justice is inevitably implicated in—and just as surely becomes buffeted by—the politics of its home state. Such organizations may start with good intentions and may well have strong grassroots connections. But they always run the very real risk of becoming a helpful initiative of the strong and rich, both locally and internationally. The relationship of the Southern NGO with its Northern donors is not egalitarian. A "community group" or a "social movement" becomes dependent on outside funding, with the inevitable consequences. Its leader, or leadership, becomes as important as the organization itself, raising problems of accountability. The organization—and others like it—has to deal with issues of poverty and human welfare during a time of a worldwide government retreat from public provision of health and education services and, in the words of a former World Bank official in Sri Lanka, a "shift of funding away from the state towards NGOs."[22]

●  ●  ●

"In a world of conflicting interests," wrote Jørgen Lissner well before the revival of civil society, challenging power relations "means making choices which are political, accepting compromises which are debatable and influencing public opinion in one direction, rather than another. In others words, helping people is a political art, just as politics is a way of helping people."[23]

And just as getting on a bus in Sri Lanka is not the same as boarding one in Canada, so civil society in two dramatically different countries is bound to be vastly different. But if civil society means citizens acting in free association, motivated by objectives other than profit-making, both the VON and Sarvodaya qualify—with important qualifications. Both occupy the space between the government and the market as non-governmental organizations; both have a basis in altruism and voluntarism. But both have become large, complex institutions, sacrificing a measure of autonomy in exchange for funding from governments (in the case of the VON) and foreign agencies (in the case of Sarvodaya). If funding completely evaporated, each would necessarily assume an entirely different form.

Like other NGOs (community organizations, women's groups, co-operatives, environmental organizations) that form part of civil society North and South, these organizations undertake implicitly political tasks. They must deal with fundamental (class, gender, ethnic) power relations that are endemic to their own societies and inherent to the architecture of their own organizations. In the end their activities—and internal structures—may only maintain these power relations or, possibly, simply obscure them. Then again, they just might take action to challenge those relations—and find a new balance.

# 3

# From Enlightenment to Globalization:
## A Historical Passage

> The welfare state is sort of like the public
> library: You use it a lot when the kids are small
> and again when you retire. But most everyone
> gets to use it.
>
> John Myles, "Inequality and Democracy," 1998

Adam Smith once expressed a certain frustration about a customary practice that, as late as 1775, stubbornly persisted in his native Scotland. Apparently there was still a village "where it is not uncommon, I am told, for a workman to carry nails instead of money to the baker's shop or the alehouse."[1]

In late eighteenth-century Britain you bought your bread and beer with cash money, or at least that's what Smith believed you should do. You did not make your own, or indulge in out-of-date customs such as barter. Capitalism's famous theorist, a keen analyst of the division of labour, believed that everything from labour to nails should be offered on the market, where money (not nails) was the preferred mode of exchange. Barter was something for backward people. Smith also argued against the primacy of agriculture, emphasizing instead a market-based system of "manufactures."

Markets are hallmarks of capitalist development. For U.S. social critic Lewis Mumford, capitalism was a cuckoo's egg laid in the nests of early European cities, destined to grow and grow until it conquered the countryside and, eventually, the world. For Walt Rostow, an economic historian specializing in English industrialization, a modern image was more appropriate for countries that were to escape backwardness and barter. Rostow described the changes in England as a "takeoff"—a plane leaving the runway.

Adam Smith (1723-90) was one of the principal ideologists of the takeoff. For Smith, writing as industrial England was starting its ascent, social life was centred on the economy and the market. Reasonable men pursued wealth through individual self-interest, free from the dictates of the mercantilist state and the trappings of feudalism. Smith argued that trade and exchange, thus liberated, had the potential to benefit everyone. The dynamic market system could be the foundation of a well-ordered society: "Little else is requisite to carry a state to the highest degree of opulence from the lowest barbarism, but peace, easy taxes, and a tolerable administration of justice; all the rest being brought about by the natural course of things. All governments which thwart this natural course, which force things into another channel, or which endeavour to arrest the progress of society at a particular point, are unnatural and to support themselves are liable to be oppressive and tyrannical."[2]

According to Smith, trade and exchange would bring vast potential gains for everyone. As Roger Scruton puts it, Smith "defended laissez-faire and believed that a market economy left to itself, while not without its evils, nevertheless has a natural tendency to equilibrium possessed by no rival economic system."[3]

Before the eighteenth century, "civil society" and "the state" were almost interchangeable terms in European thought. But civil society gradually began to be defined in opposition to the state, becoming the sphere of rights, property, and the market, a place where individuals were free to pursue their own self-interests. In the tradition of the Scottish Enlightenment, advanced nations had transcended the archaic bonds of feudalism and mercantilism and were on the road to industrial progress, or takeoff. Contracts would govern relations between people, ensuring social co-operation and exchange. The division of labour that accompanies progress of this sort would lead to increased levels of productivity. As the old saying goes, the rising tide lifts all boats. The capitalist, Smith said, is "led by an invisible hand to promote an end which was no part of his intention."[4] Self-interest inevitably contributes to the general welfare.

Since Smith's time, when the power of monarch and church was being challenged by rights-bearing individuals, the idea of civil society has gone through the Mixmaster of political theory. Distinctions between the public and the private, the civil and the political, were growing, along with a class of men whose new-found economic power was giving them autonomy from the Crown and clergy. Smith's fellow Scot Adam Ferguson (1723-1816) confronted the notion of civil society more directly. Ferguson's *Essay on the History of Civil Society* notes the "civilizing" trends in modern society. Manufacturing expands, technology improves, costs decline, and profits rise with the division of labour; orderly government moderates conflicts, facilitates contractual relationships, and hastens commercial progress. At the same time the old clan-based society of the Scottish Highlands was being ripped asunder by enclosures, clearances, and new forms of property relations. A recent editor of the *Essay* points out how Ferguson's views were shaped by the changes witnessed in Scotland in his day. "The *Essay* was the work of a man who knew intimately, and from the inside, the two civilizations (for his Lowland friends, of course, there was only one) which divided eighteenth century Scotland: the *Gemeinschaft* of the clan, belonging to the past, the *Gesellschaft* of the 'progressive' commercial lowlands."[5]

*Gemeinschaft* implies personal ties—the traditional association of kinship and community—and *Gesellschaft* impersonal ties—the modern society based on contracts and self-interest. But Ferguson was "by no means an apologist of modern progress," says John Keane, who notes that the Scot was especially concerned about:

> the matter in which civil society indices a loss of "public spirit" among its (male, property-owning) citizens. Their "disinterested love of the public" withers away; public life is considered "a scene for the gratification of mere vanity, avarice and ambition; never as furnishing the best opportunity for a just and happy engagement of the mind and heart." Chief among the causes of this corruption of public spirit is the modern division of labour. Ferguson argues that corruption was relatively absent in more simply organized "rude" (hunting and fishing) societies and in the smaller citizen states of classical Greece and the Roman republic. In modern civil societies, by contrast, the deepening division of labour—between public administration and private citizens and politicians, between entrepreneurs and workers, soldiers and civilians, corrodes the bonds of civil association.[6]

Civil society's complexity and inherent paradoxes are evident here. Ferguson apparently had minor misgivings about the new order. The rights talk of the classical theory that inspired American and French revolutionaries in their struggles against the despotisms of their day was, as Keane notes parenthetically, restricted to men of property. Peasants, workers, and women need not apply.

Nevertheless, the liberal concept of individual rights and

freedoms represents a major step forward in the history of human society. If capitalism was indeed a cuckoo's egg laid centuries ago in the nests of European cities, the medieval saying that "city air makes men free" also has considerable traction. Rights and freedoms would not long remain the sole property of the bourgeoisie. The struggles were long and the demands were firmly resisted by the wealthy and powerful, but those ideals of rights and freedoms eventually won disenfranchised peoples the right to vote. They helped to open up political space for peoples oppressed by colonialism, class, racial and gender discrimination, arbitrary imprisonment, censorship, sexual preference, disability—the list is long, and undoubtedly never-ending.

Powerful states, from monarchs and maharajahs of old to more recent authoritarian regimes both left and right, have always tended to push people around, just as men have always been inclined to treat women arbitrarily. The age of classical liberalism and civil society gave birth to one of the first manifestos questioning this supposedly natural order of things. In 1792 the English writer Mary Wollstonecraft, an admirer of the French Revolution, wrote *A Vindication of the Rights of Woman*. She put forward the (then novel) idea that women were rational beings who should throw aside the male-imposed order that held them in domestic servitude, subject to the control of husbands and fathers. Others would follow, putting the idea into action.

In the two centuries after Smith and Ferguson, human rights would become a terrain of intense struggle, with the very concept constantly contested by those who seek to maintain, or place, limits on freedom and those who seek to expand the horizons in new, more creative ways. The 1993 World Conference on Human Rights used the foundation of the

Universal Declaration of Human Rights of 1948 to push the
envelope further. Dozens of nations signed the 1993 Vienna
Declaration, which proclaims, "It is for States to foster
participation by the poorest people in the decision-making
process [and in] the promotion of human rights and efforts to
combat extreme poverty."

If classical conceptions of rights have become contested
terrain, so too has the idea of civil society itself. Its recent
revival has raised suspicions on the left. Stringent Marxists are
inclined to argue that even if we see the concept of civil society
as a key to defending human rights in general against the heavy
hand of the state, we cannot ignore its historic associations
with the specific property relations of capitalism. Whatever the
importance of dense thickets of neighbourhood associations or
freely chosen human relations outside the state and the market, the argument goes, one should not neglect class relations.
Canadian political theorist Ellen Meiksins Wood warns that
"however constructive its uses in defending human liberties
against state oppression," civil society has become a cult, an
"all-purpose catchword for the left . . . an alibi for capitalism."[7]

• • •

If Adam Smith, the father of classical economics, was the
principal ideologist of capitalism's takeoff, Karl Marx was its
principal critic—though both shared the modernist contempt
for what Marx called the "idiocy" of rural life. By the time
Marx wrote, the changes that Smith had noticed with approval
were fully underway. The mills were indeed satanic. Cities
expanded, first in England, then elsewhere, now everywhere.
What Dickens called Coketown was the most degraded
environment in the history of human creation. The old-

fashioned marketplace had given way to the growth of an efficient, superproductive market economy that was becoming global in its reach. The takeoff sprang from the factory, the railroad, the slum, and the colony. Lewis Mumford, who observed "development" through a wide-angle lens, summed up the imperatives of the nineteenth century:

> Capitalism tended to expand the province of the marketplace and turn every part of the city into a negotiable commodity. . . . The political base of this new type of urban aggregation rested on three main pillars: the abolition of the guilds and the creation of a state of permanent insecurity among the working classes: the establishment of the competitive open market for labour and for the sale of goods: the maintenance of foreign dependencies as source of raw materials, necessary to new industries, and as a ready market to absorb the surplus of mechanized industry.[8]

These very conditions caused Karl Marx to remark famously that "the philosophers" (of civil society and so on) had simply interpreted the world, but that the point was to change it. Of course, the world was already being changed willy-nilly, turned upside down by the invisible hand of the market and the highly visible hand of a state that enforced contracts and laws protecting the rights of property. Marx argued not only that civil society was "the theatre of all history," but also that it had not yet provided a place for people to free themselves.

For Marx, modern civil society was an improvement over an earlier, pre-capitalist society in which liberty was not a notion that animated the dominant class. There had been a "democracy of unfreedom." But the Marxist view, says Neera Chandhoke, held that the new civil society was "the sphere where the powerlessness of the individual in production relations is rendered opaque by the empty political rhetoric of equality and freedom."[9]

The market metaphor that still animates the globalization gospel provided Marx with the opportunity to comment on the transition to private enterprise: "He, who before was the money owner, now strides in front as capitalist; the possessor of labour power follows as his labourer. The one with an air of importance, smirking, intent on business; the other timid and holding back, like one who is bringing his own hide to market and has nothing to expect but a hiding."[10]

In this sense the market is not simply a realm of freedom and choice but also a place in which human relationships, often of the coercive variety, are moulded. Classical Marxism maintains that this system is unsustainable, that it will crumble from the weight of its internal contradictions. This has clearly not come to pass, and the post-Cold War era has brought with it a crisis in Marxist thinking. The centralized state socialism of Leninist lore, it turned out, had sharper internal contradictions than market capitalism. Aside from stifling individual freedom and civil society itself, it failed to deliver the goods on the production end of things—all the while fouling the natural environment with the abandon of a nineteenth-century robber baron.

Capitalism, though, has continued to be a galloping success, at least as far as production is concerned. Although it has shown repeatedly that it can cope very well without freedom and democracy, it has consistently proven itself ultra-resilient, able to weather the storms of economic depression and crises of political legitimacy. It is a system with built-in tendencies to inequality, with the poor and the powerless excluded both politically and materially. But it has persisted in spite of everything Marx and, later, Lenin predicted about its inevitable demise.

Meanwhile, the Leninist vision of a disciplined party guiding a workers' state collapsed in ruins, just as Enrico Malatesta had predicted immediately after the Russian Revolution. "Tomorrow, [the dictatorship of the party] will help impose the dictators' will on the people, stop the revolution, consolidate and defend new interests of a new privileged class against the masses," the Italian anarchist wrote in 1919.[11] When the leader of the Soviet communists died five years later, Malatesta was quick to suggest that Lenin's demise be celebrated as a popular holiday.*

By that time the Italian communists, often an unconventional lot, had already founded their own party under the leadership of Antonio Gramsci, who would soon be jailed by the Italian fascists. Gramsci spent the rest of his life in prison, where he had ample time to reflect on why the demise of capitalism had not happened, as his Marxist texts had indicated it would. The Italian intellectual came up with the concept of *hegemony* to describe the complex and often hidden ways in which class domination seeps into social institutions, becoming particularly pervasive in advanced capitalist societies. The term derived from the Greek *hegemon*, indicating a man who was the leader or "chief ruler," often of more than just his own state. (Hegemony has been used to describe Great Power influence, as in the hegemony of Athens in Ancient Greece or, more recently, British hegemony in the Indian subcontinent or U.S. hegemony in Latin America.)

Gramsci was concerned about the unequal relations, not between states, but between social classes. He examined the predominance of bourgeois hegemony, a state of affairs in which the ideology of the dominant class becomes the accepted common sense of society, legitimizing the overweening power of the market and those who control its key institutions.

---

* Many revolutions, from 1789 in France to Russia in 1917, China in 1949, and Cuba in 1959, have neutralized the social forces that originally backed them and gone on to prevent wherever possible the re-establishment of independent citizen initiatives.

Gramsci's contribution underlined the importance of class rule as something that extends beyond the economy to the spheres of politics and culture. Schools, religious congregations, unions, hospitals, farmers' associations, "community" groups—most of which have come to constitute what policy analysts and NGOs regard as civil society—are in Gramscian terms all profoundly influenced by the logic that it is somehow part of the natural order of things for one class to maintain influence over less powerful classes. "The idea of **hegemony**," explains Raymond Williams, is "especially important in societies in which electoral politics and public opinion are significant factors, and in which social practice is seen to depend on consent to certain dominant ideas which in fact express the needs of a dominant class."[12]

Civil society is bound up with the state, not only defined as the formal machinery of government but also as the apparatus of "hegemony or civil society." According to Chandhoke, Gramscian civil society is a place, or places.

> What Gramsci does is to bring to our attention the fact that in capitalist societies power is diffused at various sites, and takes various forms. He spatially relocates the site of consent and, thereby, of the domination of the ruling classes. . . . Civil society is the location where the state operates to enforce invisible, intangible and subtle forms of power, through educational, cultural and religious systems and other institutions. The political society disciplines the body through its penal codes and prisons, but civil society disciplines the mind and the psyche through these institutions.[13]

According to this analysis, capitalism tends to be most stable in countries with highly developed civil societies. Looking back at his own era, Gramsci saw that Western Europe had a huge working class, the *sine qua non* for revolution, at least according to classical Marxist theory. Russia had neither highly developed civil society nor a big proletariat. It did have a revolution in the tumultuous period at the end of World War I. The twentieth-century revolutions that followed—China, Cuba, Vietnam, Nicaragua—all took place in peasant societies and dressed themselves as much in anti-colonialist and nationalist garb as they did in socialist colours. In such lands a complex array of prefeudal, feudal, and capitalist social relations indigenous to Southern lands (Adam Ferguson's "rude" societies) had been disrupted by colonialism. As the architecture of traditional civil society (religious organizations, informal networks promoting local self-sufficiency, councils of village elders, market-women's associations) evolved, it was shaped by both colonial—and, later, postcolonial—states as well as the imperatives of the market. Meanwhile, in the industrial North, similar forces were shaping an intricate web of civil society organizations ("ladies' auxiliaries" both formal and informal, Boy Scout troops, teachers' unions, associations of hospital administrators).

• • •

When Antonio Gramsci wrote about civil society, the West was on the verge of a catastrophic depression that was followed by world war, cold war, and a "long boom" lasting until the 1970s. Indeed, it was only when that boom was petering out that discussions of civil society were again taken up in seminar rooms frequented by left-wing intellectuals.* They

---

* The work of Gramsci, arguably the greatest Marxist thinker of the century, became influential not just because he contributed to the understanding of capitalism's staying power; intellectuals also revere the Italian radical because he saw intellectuals playing a central role in social transformation.

also found their way into the smoky cafés of Prague and Budapest, the bars of Rio de Janeiro and Buenos Aires, and, eventually, the swank offices of the World Bank. Along the way, they filtered into the more modest premises in which many NGOs ponder the possibilities of fresh approaches to empowering the poor.

The period from the late 1920s to the mid-1970s did not witness the neglect of civil society simply because Gramsci's writings were only translated into English some thirty-five years after he died in Mussolini's prison in 1937. It was a time when most political thinking understandably concentrated on the role of the state. Fascist states held sway in Germany, Italy, Spain, and Portugal. Japan had a monarchy. Sundry oligarchies prevailed in Latin America. Autocratic colonial states ruled much of the South until nationalists forced the British to quit India, starting the process that would put an end to formal empire. After the Second World War, authoritarian state socialism still prevailed in the Soviet Union. Indeed, it had spread to China and, in the eyes of the planners of empire, threatened to engulf much of the rest of the globe. Meanwhile the ideas of John Maynard Keynes had taken hold in the centres of advanced industrial capitalism. The effects of the Great Depression of the 1930s thoroughly discredited classical market economics, and Keynes's state-centred approach supplanted laissez-faire. The Bretton Woods accords of 1944, much influenced by Keynes, recognized that nation-states had the right to control the movement of capital. Keynes also believed that high unemployment and low wages—conditions always close to the hearts of employers—reduced demand. Under Keynesian policies, governments got into the business of attacking unemployment by stimulating demand, in part through public works. Northern welfare-state programs—and welfare-state industries such as the health and education facilities that exploded in size after World War II—were a critical ingredient of the Keynesian recipe.

In the postcolonial South, the state also had pride of place during this period. Nationalist leaders who inherited the administrative apparatus from imperial powers, inspired by visions of industrial modernity, used a *dirigiste* model of "development," complete with public works, massive megaprojects, and five-year plans. Government also zealously guarded national security against threats from outside invaders or internal agitators. Postcolonial politicians lavished scarce funds on the new military establishments of their new nations, often only to find that the officer corps seized power for itself. Along the way the appetite for national security encouraged the growth of an international arms trade.

In Nehru's India, although the military did not intrude into politics as in neighbouring Pakistan, and the ruling Congress Party did not administer a command economy on the Soviet or Chinese model, the government did become heavily involved in finance and industry. The goal was strong domestic manufacturing, partly state-owned but with significant involvement of the domestic capitalists who benefited from interventionist government policies. Huge firms such as Tata and Birla went forth and prospered. Agriculture remained overwhelmingly in private hands.

By the 1990s the situation in India had changed, as it had throughout the South. With the end of the Cold War and the rise of a neo-classical economic thinking that privileges the market above all else, a heavily indebted state found itself under attack, both within and without. That pattern was repeated throughout the South. "India must be opened up!" urged *The Economist*, a publication that would see Hollywood,

Colonel Sanders, and Barclay's Bank as ideal tools for breaching protectionist walls. The view from the bottom was rather different. Any such "opening up" would most likely not alter a situation in which affluent landlords and other assorted bosses enjoyed the protection of corrupt government officials. "It may be the case that state-directed planning has enabled the private sector in India to grow strong enough to find the extensive public sector the main impediment to its further profitable expansion," observed Ramesh Thakur.[14]

Whatever the reasons, by the 1980s the state was falling into bad odour. The debt crisis had led to structural adjustment programs imposed on Southern states by the International Monetary Fund and World Bank. Governments were instructed to reduce their minimal welfare programs, including the price supports for basic fuel and foodstuffs that helped the most vulnerable people. The market was thenceforth to be the pathway to prosperity for all, rich and poor. This neo-liberal offensive, driven in part by the Reagan and Thatcher regimes in the United States and United Kingdom respectively, derived from the world view originally inspired by Adam Smith and the classical economists. Market fundamentalism had always been central to capitalist ideology. It had merely been overshadowed (outside the Communist bloc) during the brief interlude lasting from the 1930s to the 1970s. This historical hiccup came to an end when a surprised Keynesianism came up against an increasingly serious fiscal crisis of the state. Anyone who believed that the state was central to serious efforts at reducing inequality or that it might be a good idea to place constraints on the unlimited freedom of capital was pushed onto the defensive.

During the postwar period the examples of the "actually existing socialism" in the Soviet bloc and China were crucial to the geopolitical architecture of the era. As long as a Red Threat existed, non-aligned Southern governments could benefit from superpower rivalry. Despite its gulags and its secret police, state socialism had for decades offered the possibility that there just might be another road to "development." But by the 1970s the decay in the Soviet bloc was clearly evident. In some countries (the USSR itself, Hungary, Poland) life expectancy—a key social indicator—had stagnated and even declined in the two decades before the Berlin Wall was smashed into a pile of prized tourist curios.[15] The Soviet bloc could not always deliver the goods to citizens deprived of any political or social space not controlled by the party and the state. Public life was marked by a corrosive cynicism over a political system rife with cronyism and corruption. Still, some citizens did make efforts, often small and unacknowledged, to resist the despotism of the party-state apparatus. They fashioned informal networks with others who shared their commitment to freedom of thought. They published *samizdat*, organized discussion groups, and struggled to create independent professions and unions, creating spaces in which freedom could take root.

The renewed interest in civil society coincided roughly with the decline of state socialism. The concept itself became widely associated with dissident intellectuals and their critiques of the Stalinist order. Indeed, the recent blizzard of writing about civil society usually attributes to Eastern European thinkers a major role in the reintroduction of the term to political discussions. "It is undeniably the case," observed Krishan Kumar, that the example of these activist thinkers "has inspired several western thinkers to reconsider the concept of civil society."[16]

In 1976 a group of fourteen Polish intellectuals established the Workers' Defence Committee (KOR), an organization that within four years had evolved into a mass opposition movement existing outside the official, state-sponsored structures of political life. KOR generated a lively underground *samizdat* press and, along with Poland's immensely powerful Catholic church, paved the way for the growth of the mass-based Solidarity opposition. KOR's example emboldened other dissident forces, forcing the state to tolerate the existence of an increasingly lively opposition. Jacek Kuron, a key KOR leader, advocated direct democracy and, as part of this, "different self-managements; different cultural associations . . . an organized farmers' movement, a movement of citizens' initiatives, of discussion clubs designed to work out different concepts, centers whose task it would be to integrate individual programs. And, of course, also unions."[17]

Such revisioning of democracy helped to revitalize political life in Poland, liberating it from the stranglehold of the party-state. In Hungary a narrower opposition was aided by reform Communists. The East German opposition got a late start and never amounted to much of a threat to a regime armed with a hyper-efficient security apparatus. Repression was also strong in Czechoslovakia, where the well-known Charter 77 group never aspired to the status of a serious mass movement. So although throughout Eastern and Central Europe there was a role for intellectuals who thought about civil society as a site of opposition, Michael Bernhard has concluded that Poland "remains the only unambiguous case" in the region. In Poland "an opposition, not assisted by regime-sponsored liberalization, created an extensive public space on a national level on the basis of its own power and successfully maintained its boundaries vis-a-vis the state through practices of social self-defense."[18]

Even before the trade union Solidarity had emerged as a serious opposition force, Czech intellectual Jacques Rupnik described the situation in Poland as "the end of revisionism and the rebirth of civil society."[19] However, when the end of state socialism finally came in the second half of 1989, it was not due to a upsurge animated by a vibrant network of civil society organizations. The Berlin Wall and the statues of Lenin and Stalin came down only because no Eastern European government had the will to order the troops to administer Napoleon's famous "whiff of grapeshot" when the time came. (The Chinese authorities had exhibited no such compunctions at Tiananmen Square several months earlier.) Tens of thousands did take to the streets, and there was no stopping those who demolished the most potent symbols of Camus' observation about Stalinist totalitarianism: "Nowhere in the world has there been a party or a man with absolute power who did not use it absolutely."[20]

The regimes, lacking any popular legitimacy and uncertain that their absolute power was ensured by the Soviets, collapsed on their own account. It was clear to all concerned that Mikhail Gorbachev's Soviet Union would no longer offer armoured divisions to party officials in satellite states. Instead the advice from Moscow was to follow a flexible line. "None of the regimes in Eastern Europe were *over-thrown*," emphasized historian Eric Hobsbawm, who has studied the nineteenth century and its revolutions.

> They were replaced, briefly, by the men and (once again, far too rarely) women who had represented dissidence or opposition, and who had organized, or perhaps better, successfully called for the mass demonstrations which gave the signal for the old regimes' peaceful abdication. Except in Poland, where Church and the trade unions formed the backbone of opposition, they consisted of a few often very brave intellectuals, a stage-army of leaders which briefly found itself at the head of peoples. . . . There was a tidal wave of talk about "civil society," i.e. the ensemble of

voluntary citizens' organizations or private activities, taking
the place of authoritarian states, and about the return to the
principles of revolutions before Bolshevism had distorted
them. Alas, as in 1848, the moment of freedom and truth
did not last. . . . The *ad hoc* "fronts" or "civic movements"
crumbled as rapidly as they had risen.[21]

Whatever the fate of civil society in the Eastern bloc (it would
emerge as being more dynamic in, say, the Czech Republic and
Hungary than in the Soviet Union), by the time the Berlin wall
came down and the Soviet Union had faded as a geopolitical
force, the term was back in vogue both West (or, in "development" terms, the North) and South. A new kind of revolution
was apparently gathering momentum, the "global associational
revolution" comprising innumerable, independent private
associations "not dedicated to distributing profits to share-
holders or directors" but promoting the public good "outside
the formal apparatus of the state."[22]

• • •

The new popularity of NGOs and "civil society" has emerged
against a background of major shifts in the world system.
Conditions have changed dramatically since the Cold War, the
rise of the notion of "underdevelopment," and the aid enterprise took hold in the early 1950s. With the end of the Cold
War, which was such an important spur to the development
enterprise, the geopolitical situation altered. The fall of authoritarian state socialism and the command economies of the
Soviet bloc was accompanied by the emergence of (formerly
"Red") China as market opportunity and a source of low-wage
labour. Once a threat, China now represents—at least according to the editors of *The Economist*—"some of the biggest

business and financial opportunities in history." The arrival of modernity in "middle-class" Asia ("they will be buying houses, cars, holidays, health care and education . . .") came to be regarded, at least before the 1997 meltdown, with unalloyed bliss by business commentators.[23]

The end of the Cold War was preceded by the fiscal crisis of the state in the West. The postwar "long boom" began a long decline in 1973. Donor nations have recently made major cuts to their aid budgets, spending that is far more politically vulnerable than welfare-state services ("houses, health care, education"), which have nonetheless also been seriously eroded. The citizens of donor nations have been told repeatedly that austerity is here to stay, that unemployment rates of 10 per cent at the top of the business cycle are the norm, that they will have to lower their expectations.

There has also been an ideological shift marked by the return of nineteenth-century laissez-faire values. Market ideology is impelled by a belief in the paramount position of individual consumer choice. According to this view the state is best restricted to enforcing contracts and ensuring that the police maintain order. As many functions as possible should be deregulated, privatized, left to the market.

Finally, two shifts have taken place with regard to the division of labour. A new international division of labour resulted in a southward shift of both light and heavy manufacturing. While donor nations ponder the meaning of the term "rust belt," many Southern countries have seen an explosion in manufacturing, which has been accompanied by equally rapid urbanization. The division of labour between humans and machines continues to tilt in favour of the latter. "It's not Mexico," Merton Miller of the University of Chicago advised that city's anxious packinghouse and steel workers, "it's the machine." From the other side of the ideological fence, Marxist historian Hobsbawm pointed out that even the newly industrial countries "were governed by the iron logic of mechanization, which sooner or later made even the cheapest human being more expensive than a machine."[24] The effect of all of this was to enhance the bargaining power of capital over labour.

Nations, regions, and even small cities queue up to offer corporations the best tax breaks and incentives in exchange for an assembly plant or a call centre. It's a buyer's market often tilted in favour of countries whose comparative advantage lies in their low labour costs. This edge is not necessarily confined to textiles or even heavy industry. The research arm of BCE, one of Canada's largest conglomerates and a world telecommunications leader, has contracted low-wage (by Canadian standards) software engineers in Bangalore to perform the work of testing S/DMS TransportNode transmission systems. The company calls this "sharing information and resources between . . . geographically dispersed design teams . . . to create a seamless global R&D community."[25]

Together with other trends, such as the increased mobility of deregulated financial capital and the spread of an American-style commercial culture of entertainment and mass consumption (Ivan Illich remarked that thirst had been translated into the need for a Coke), these developments have congealed into what is now commonly called globalization. There is apparently a new world order in which national states are becoming increasingly helpless vis-à-vis transnational corporations and fast-moving finance. The message is constantly repeated: we have entered a radically new phase, with the international economy more open than it has ever been. Moreover—and this is the political edge of the globalization hypothesis—we are told there is little we can do—no matter our concerns—but submit to the imperatives of the competitive market.

A transformed geopolitical environment. The relentless march of technological change. Shifts in the ideological wind. An increasingly deregulated economy. A changing political geography. This is the backdrop for discussions of civil society—that fuzzy space between the state and the market—at international conferences, academic chin-wags, and NGO policy-gatherings. But globalization, particularly the internationalization of the economy, is not new. And the social relations of production and exchange between—and within—nations that developed with the rise of capitalism have not changed fundamentally with the introduction of computers, satellites, or the establishment of intricate rules of trade as embodied now by the World Trade Organization. Indeed, in relation to GNP, capital flows were larger in the period leading up to 1914 than they were in the 1980s. As Paul Hirst and Grahame Thompson argue in *Globalization in Question*, the economic integration of recent years is the result of conscious policy decisions, particularly the abandonment of controls on the free movement of capital. This is a complex issue, linked to the demise of the controls of the Bretton-Woods regime. Major nation-states (and increasingly distinct power blocs dominated by particular states) determine the structure of the international economy and the distribution of power within it. According to Hirst and Thompson the globalization argument is essentially political in that, once the notion of an ungovernable world economy is accepted as gospel—as it is in many business and political circles—the result is a paralysis of "radical reforming national strategies." New forms of regulation or governance come to be seen as impossible in the face of "the judgement and sanction of international markets."

(Markets have come to take on human characteristics, making judgements and decisions. Once this mindset is established, one can easily forget that markets—and market relations—are social creations.)

Hirst and Thompson point to the long postwar boom and its demise as a key factor in the increased traction enjoyed by the globalization argument, which, they say, has emerged as "a response to the collapse of expectations schooled by Keynesianism and sobered by the failure of monetarism." Referring to the political impact of globalization as "the pathology of over-diminished expectations," Hirst and Thompson argue that globalization is "a necessary myth." They do not claim that important changes have not taken place in the world economy, particularly since 1973. But increased "inter-nationalization" should not be mistaken for immutable globalization.[26]

Globalization is a necessary myth because it provokes a sense of political paralysis among those who might otherwise imagine alternatives to an unstable world economy dominated by currency speculators and transnational capital. In this global world, according to UN Secretary-General Kofi Annan's statement to the In Common campaign sponsored by Canadian NGOs, 1.3 billion people (a third of the population of the South) live on less than a dollar a day. Where 515 million people in South Asia alone live in poverty. Where the prices of the commodities that support the poorest countries have been 45 per cent lower in the 1990s than they were in the 1980s—and 10 per cent lower than they were in 1932 in the depths of the Great Depression. Where the terms of trade of the least developed countries have dropped by a cumulative 50 per cent in the past twenty-five years. Where the poorest 20 per cent of the globe's people now receive 1.1 per cent of its income, down from 2.3 per cent in 1960. Where, according to the UN's

*Human Development Report*, "the greatest benefits of global-ization have been garnered by a fortunate few".[27]

Northern societies (in particular the United States, which has, according to the World Bank, higher levels of income inequality than do many nations of the South)[28] are character-ized by increasing levels of social exclusion and a growing feel-ing that social bonds are being ruptured. In the North a grow-ing surplus of workers exists in a service sector increasingly conquered by computers. Financial services need fewer people to process transactions. Retailing is becoming more concen-trated. A contingent workforce combs the labour market in search of part-time and contract jobs, giving rise to the bizarre paradox of a population living in a time of unprecedented abundance but at the same time increasingly anxious about the material future.

The market system has always had a tendency to overcapacity. There is another paradox here. A global surplus of everything from food to videos co-exists with hundreds of millions of people living in destitution. Not only that, but over-capacity breeds economic instability. The familiar historical cycle of boom and bust has not suddenly vanished in the era of globalization. If anything, the international economy is more unstable than ever. According to Richard Barnet and John Cavanagh:

> The surplus of gifted, skilled, undervalued, and unwanted human beings is the Achilles heel of this emerging global sys-tem. The problem is starkly simple: An astonishingly large and increasing number of people are not needed or wanted to make the goods or to provide the services that the paying customers of the world can afford. The gathering pressures of global competition to cut costs threaten the vast majority of the 8 billion human beings expected to be living on earth in the first quarter of the next century with the prospect that they will be neither producers nor consumers.[29]

What we have here is, all in all, not a terribly bright picture of the global world order. But again, problems of poverty and exclusion are scarcely new. In 1960 an idealistic Canadian aid official touring South Asia was so shocked by the appalling conditions in which "the vast majority of Asians are condemned to live and die" that he told his superiors "not a penny nor a minute can be spared for any purpose that does not lead directly to a permanent and measurable diminution of poverty."[30] Yet development assistance (or "external aid") was in those days strictly a matter of trickle-down growth and modernization—the bigger the infrastructure project the better. Hence Canada's eagerness to build dams in South Asia. Although those times had a place for idealism, the dominant view held that "authentic idealism seeks above all the workable—the realistic. In the practice of foreign policy, idealism consists of choosing the most effective means of advancing the nation's interest, broadly and imaginatively understood."[31]

The aid enterprise in the era of globalization has certainly changed, but it remains an uneasy blend of altruism and *realpolitik*. So it is too with the notion of "civil society" that has become pervasive in the vocabulary of policy entrepreneurs within that regime—and well beyond.

# 4

# "As Long as People Are People":
# Voluntarism, Government, and Politics

> As long as people are people, democracy, in
> the full sense of the word, will always be no
> more than an ideal. One may approach it as
> one would the horizon in ways that may be
> better or worse, but it can never be fully
> attained. In this sense, you, too, are merely
> approaching democracy.
>
> Václav Havel, Czech Republic president, addressing the
> U.S. Congress, 1990

The week after the fall of the Berlin wall, the shrewd American
cartoonist Garry Trudeau portrayed conflicting interpretations
of the historic event. For one of his principal characters, the
idealistic Mark Slackmeyer, the symbolic fall of communism
was a victory for the human spirit. Mark's hard-boiled father
viewed it differently.

"It's over," the businessman declared. "We won."

Efforts to interpret the end of the Soviet bloc went well
beyond the comics. At a scholarly conference in 1996, political
scientist Katherine Fierlbeck presented a paper titled
"Fetishizing Civil Society."

"The Cold War is over," the Canadian academic declared. "Locke is the victor."[1]

The implication is that the end of socialism as we knew it signalled a triumph for the world view expounded three centuries ago by Englishman John Locke, the early modern political theorist and father of liberalism who argued that government should concern itself mainly with enforcing contracts and property rights. Locke's idea was revolutionary at the time. Locke himself observed that new opinions (like his own) were usually unpopular, opposed simply by virtue of their novelty. But by the late twentieth century Locke's approach had become thoroughly fashionable. A minimal state is the most desirable state. The state concerns itself with balancing budgets, quelling inflation, and cutting taxes. Market relations intrude into everyday life, creating opportunities for profit at every possible turn. Commercialized services abound, offering to care for your elderly parents or to sell you the very latest in software because the computer program you purchased eigteen months back is now so out of date that it is allegedly useless. The largest firms even claim patent rights on the genetic properties of seeds and traditional medicines. Those who doubt that all of this is possible need look no further than the assertion once wielded by idealists concerned with stopping environmental degradation or narrowing the gap between the rich and poor: "It *is* possible." The phrase has been trademarked by the Bank of Montreal as part of an advertising campaign to convince people of the merits of electronic banking.

If the Cold War is over and we (or Locke) won, what now? Real wages of the average Canadian worker dropped by 5 per cent between 1990 and 1996, with those in the lowest quintile experiencing a 19 per cent decline.[2] The number of Canadians using food banks more than doubled between 1989 and 1997.[3] In the latter year the Bank of Montreal's chief executive officer received a pay increase of 8 per cent, bringing his total compensation to $4.2 million.[4] Canada's banking industry, already highly concentrated, began a process of further consolidation designed, customers were told, to meet the new era of global competition. The merger move, halted at least temporarily by a public outcry, would have reduced jobs, branches, and competition in the domestic market.

*Fin de siècle* Americans realize that their long experiment with expanding mass prosperity is at an end. By the late 1980s, after-tax median incomes were well below those of the late 1970s. The top 10 per cent of households controlled a stunning 68 per cent of the nation's wealth. The term millionaire no longer referred to someone with a million dollars but someone with an annual *income* of over a million dollars. Workers who had shared the productivity dividends of the postwar golden age clearly no longer did so. Union membership as a proportion of non-agricultural employment declined steadily from a high of 32.5 per cent during the postwar boom in 1953 to 15.1 per cent in 1992.[5] The gap between the rich and the rest steadily widened. Despite the wealth and galloping modernity that still make the United States the destination of choice for would-be immigrants from around the world, the country has become remarkably fractured. For former Nixon adviser Kevin Phillips, a perceptive observer of American politics, the conclusion is inescapable: "Among major western nations, the United States has displayed one of the sharpest cleavages between rich and poor."[6]

When conventional solutions appear to be wanting, frustrated people grope about for new ideas. In 1997 U.S. community development advocate Alan AtKisson predicted, "When collapses of any kind occur, civil society will be there to pick up the pieces and rebuild. When transformation occurs, civil society will undoubtedly have hatched it. It's all but inevitable: democracy will give birth to sustainability and civil society will save the world."[7] Declaring his candidacy for the leadership of a major Canadian political party, Hugh Segal advocated reducing as much as possible the size and cost of government. He announced, "A new time . . . requires a Conservative party that embraces fiscal discipline, economic growth, free enterprise and productivity as instruments that help us strengthen the safety net that sustains our civil society."[8]

Social democrat Bob Rae, in a 1998 book, draws on U.S. political theorist Francis Fukuyama in his discussion—not of civil society—but of civil societies. This puts the emphasis on the adjective, in the same way that Segal does. For Rae civil societies are plural, with a free press, multiple centres of power, lots of voluntary organizations, an independent judiciary. They involve rights of property and the rights of individuals. "Civil societies, as their name implies, are based on a respect for public order, as well as a civility of discourse," he says.[9]

But then Professor Ted Morton, a political scientist at the University of Calgary, headed something called the Alberta Civil Society Association in 1998. The Association spent thousands of dollars on television and radio ads protesting a Supreme Court decision giving equal protection to gays and lesbians under Alberta's human rights code. The campaign was part of an angry backlash against same-sex rights that provoked heated debate on radio hotline shows and in newspaper columns. The discourse was anything but civil. All of which led Murray Billett, who spoke up for the gay community during the bitter debate, to wonder aloud, "Why do they hate us?"[10]

• • •

Ill fares the land, to hast'ning ills a prey
Where wealth accumulates, and men decay.

The lines from the Irish poet Oliver Goldsmith in his 1770 poem *The Deserted Village* were a comment on the effects of the enclosures, the appropriation of common land and its transformation into private property. The process, which turned what had long been open areas used by everyone—the people in common—into enclosed fields (often used for sheep), had accelerated dramatically in Britain by the eighteenth century. Those who benefited from the enclosures, landlords who supported the emerging system of property relations dictated not by custom but by the market, preached the gospel according to Locke: this was the true and only path to prosperity—even though it destroyed the subsistence economy of the rural poor who had relied on common lands. The elites of the day maintained that there was no alternative, while various Levellers and Luddites objected to the undemocratic nature of political representation and the vast gulf separating landless labourers from the wealth of the upper classes. Historian E.P. Thompson called the new order "a plain enough case of class robbery, played according to fair rules of property and law laid down by a parliament of property-owners and lawyers."[11]

At the end of the twentieth century, Canadians concerned about increasing inequality—or insecurity, or cleaning up the environment, or the erosion of public health care—are again being told by powerful pragmatists that there are no alternatives to the ethos of the free market; to governments hamstrung in the face of international capital markets; to the erosion of prosperity and job security; to a world with lots of problems but few if any solutions. Citizens who think that it is still possible to alter this course get angry with elected representatives unable or unwilling to do anything about shrinking incomes, public provision of health and education, and opportunities for decent jobs.

Angus Reid is one of Canada's leading pollsters, a postmodern oracle-for-hire who works for political parties, media outlets, governments, corporations, and non-profit organizations eager to take the pulse of Canadian society. In a rambling book advertised as "an urgent wake-up call to all Canadians," Reid describes the end of regulation and Keynesian capitalism and the rise of neo-liberalism as a move from a "spend-and-share" era to a more individualistic "sink-or-swim" ethic. The polls show a widespread popular disenchantment with politics. Statistics show decreasing real incomes for most citizens, accompanied by private-sector productivity increases. The times have brought rising household debt and declining welfare-state services, particularly in the universal public health-care system that Canadians have always seen as differentiating them from the United States. High levels of unemployment persist at the top of the business cycle. Jobs are clear-cut in the face of the need to be "competitive."

Angus Reid, who shares the elite consensus that "governments at all levels are essentially bankrupt and in decline," explores these troubling trends, and many more. He even extends conventional wisdom to the claim that "the state is essentially bankrupt, and under attack for having tried to take care of too many people in easier times." At the same time the pollster notes paradoxically that "voters don't want to hear about things that can't be fixed." In other words, government is powerless to do anything about the things that worry people, but the same people get mad when they hear that nothing can be done about this state of affairs, at least by the government. All of this has led to the rise of new parties and a widely recognized volatility among the electorate. As Reid states, "Canada's political traditions are now swirling around in the wind. . . . The flow of income out of the pockets of workers and into the pockets of entrepreneurs and investors will lead to more frustration at the polls, and elsewhere." Reid concludes his troubling account with the observation that, despite the many worrisome trends, Canadians remain committed to a society fundamentally different from that of the United States and "a core belief in the importance of a civil society."[12]

The vocabulary here is worth noting. Reid is a Ph.D. who makes his living analysing Canadian society. Conservative politician Hugh Segal is a shrewd observer of politics in that society. Both use the term "civil society" in a positive way, as a concrete condition of our world, and not as a form of social space. Similarly, on the day before Bill Clinton was impeached by a bitterly divided House of Representatives a Canadian journalist reporting on the acrimonious Washington scene concluded: "Impeachment is only part of the story, however. It is symptomatic of the coarsening of public life in the United States, an erosion of civility." He described a political system scarred by "poison, cynicism and apathy."[13]

The concept of civil society doesn't seem to have much to do with the theories of Adam Ferguson and Antonio Gramsci, or even with reports from the World Bank or CIVICUS.* A civil

---

* CIVICUS describes itself as "The World Alliance for Citizen Participation . . . an alliance of organizations and individuals to strengthen citizen action and influence throughout the world through voluntary initiatives, philanthropy and community service." From the back cover of Isagani Serrano, *Civil Society in the Asia-Pacific Region* (Washington: CIVICUS, 1994).

society is popularly equated with civility, or politeness, and English-Canadians see themselves as being more polite, more civil, than their counterparts in the loud, brash, gun-toting U.S.A. Indeed, we often hear suggestions that one of the important things that constitutes English Canada as a distinct society is that it is not the United States. "Civility" is clearly important here.

So too is the notion of "community," which has become a kind of shorthand for civil society to the extent that it is invoked as a way of dealing with the crisis of the welfare state during a time when increasing numbers of poor people are excluded from participation in both the labour market and other aspects of social life. While the term "participation"— which animated the new left of the 1960s and NGOs in the 1970s and 1980s—has been embraced by powerful institutions and governments worldwide (the World Bank has eighteen flagship participation projects), the idea of social exclusion has become a way of naming the inequality that characterizes Northern societies.[14] If government cannot provide remedies for exclusion, and if the salve of economic growth and laissez-faire prescribed by free-market fundamentalists has failed to engage or even assist the excluded, people from all sides turn to something called "the community." That word reached its nadir for me when I heard someone refer to "the public relations community." Community, explains Raymond Williams, "can be the warmly persuasive word to describe an existing set of relationships, or the warmly persuasive word to describe an alternative set of relationships. What is most important, perhaps, is that unlike all other terms of social organization (*state, nation, society,* etc.) it seems never to be used unfavourably, and never to be given any positive opposing or distinguishing term."[15]

Nowadays government agencies and the private sector advocate "partnerships" with community groups to address everything from hunger to support for the arts. Those advocating social justice attempt to rally the community, claiming to speak on its behalf, advocating community economic development. All of this, however, happens at the periphery of a world dominated by the market. Theologian Gregory Baum asks important questions about community endeavour: "Is this indeed an alternative, small-scale, imaginative economy that opens the way to a more democratic and communitarian social life? Or is this movement not simply a form of self-managed poverty subsidized by the state in order to appease the recriminations of those who are at the margins of society?"[16]

Sociologist Deena White has analysed "the community management of exclusion." Faced with levels of begging and homelessness formerly only associated with countries in the South, as well as pressure from financial markets to cut spending, governments in Canada turn to voluntary organizations, "desperately championing community alternatives to their own public programs." But what, she asks, is this community? Pragmatic groups of individual citizens addressing problems through voluntary associations? New forms of social relations different from those that dominate bureaucratized, capitalist society? A mere invention, "dressed in nostalgic rhetoric for consumption by those disenchanted by the perils of modernity"?

For White, community organizations (as distinct from market and state organizations) cannot meaningfully address the exclusion of growing numbers of citizens whose participation in economic life is akin to the experience of extras on a movie set—people who, for a small fee, wait around hour after hour to be called upon temporarily and who are then sent back to wait for another call. Rather than reintegrating people, the community sector risks becoming a palliative: "Current workers are being herded into the 'periphery' of part-time, temporary or contractual labour in order to augment flexibility, which makes access even to that marginal sector increasingly competitive. In this context, the community sector is inevitably coming to be seen less as a partner in the strategic countering of exclusionary forces, and more as a straightforward expansion of the economic periphery."[17]

The most obvious Canadian example of this tendency is "workfare," the new, coercive face of the welfare state. After cutting social assistance benefits by 21 per cent, the Ontario government introduced a workfare law to force poor people to take "community placements" with organizations in the voluntary sector. Other examples of "mandated" (or non-voluntary) volunteerism include sentencing people convicted of crimes to "community service" instead of prison and the growing tendency of schools and colleges to insist on volunteer activity as a condition of graduation.

Whatever the merits of these policies, they blur more than ever the boundaries between the state and community groups (the voluntary sector). Governments backing such schemes display little understanding of the voluntary sector. They force unskilled, often unwilling, labour onto organizations that have few resources to train or supervise them, at a time when such organizations are already under pressure from diminished state funding, increased competition for charitable donations from the general public, and the usual pressures to recruit and train volunteers.

Government in Canada is seeking to restructure the welfare state by offloading responsibilities, turning them over to the market, with privatization offering business the opportunity to provide services previously furnished by the public sector. This happens alongside decentralization, the offloading of responsibilities to lower levels of government that have fewer powers to tax and determine fiscal and monetary policy. Finally, partnership with the voluntary sector means arranging for non-profit community groups to provide public services on a contract basis.

Aside from saving money, the rationale behind turning to the voluntary sector is that community groups are smaller and more flexible than state bureaucracies, and better attuned to local needs. While this is true in theory, benign-sounding "partnerships" are most often contract relationships in which the state sets the rules. As this contracting regime develops, non-profit organizations may be forced to emphasize competition, a value usually associated with the market. Non-profit community groups find themselves devoting scarce time and energy to vying with each other (or, in the case of the VON, with the private sector) for contracts. This tendency will gradually transform the sector. The benign spontaneity and the grassroots, neighbourhood character that is the stuff of communitarian lore will give way to a formalized professionalism in which the latest management techniques overshadow the original community orientation.

Community organizations may confront certain difficulties in dealing with the brave new world of civil society. Half of Canada's voluntary groups operate on budgets of less than $50,000, and 60 per cent have only one full-time staff person or no staff at all.[18] These many small organizations may not have the resources to compete in an emerging partnership regime. The economics of the time may work against them. It has often been the case, as researchers Jane Jenson and Susan Phillips point out, that "once a partnership arrangement has been established and a clientele has become dependent upon it, the state's contribution to the contract is cut significantly."

Under the prevailing pressures the distinctions between civil society, on the one hand, and the market, on the other, can blur. The response to state withdrawal may well be, as Jenson and Phillips argue, "not a growth in voluntary activity but a rise in commercialism." According to these two authors: "Voluntary organizations turn to user fees and other sources of market income, thereby becoming more business-like and more integrated into the private market economy. In addition, for-profit firms begin to seek out this niche, often gradually crowding out the voluntary organizations."[19]

In 1995 and 1996 the Social Planning Council of Metropolitan Toronto conducted comprehensive surveys of community-based social service agencies. The study revealed a "system in turmoil" in which many agencies had been forced to increase demands on staff and spend more time trying to raise money from new sources and beating the bushes for more volunteers. The 293 agencies that provided budget information had lost nearly $19 million, which included $11 million less from government. The authors calculated that to make up this shortfall community groups would have needed to increase fundraising revenues by half. In fact, their fundraising declined by $8 million. The survey concluded that immigrants and refugees lost the most in terms of access to services and that other vulnerable groups (low-income families, victims of abuse, and people with disabilities) were significantly harmed by the withdrawal of community supports.[20]

One response to the voluntary sector's increasingly urgent crisis is to recycle managerial notions that have faded from fashion in the private sector. In 1998 the Donner Foundation began paying the right-wing Fraser Institute to administer something called the Donner Canadian Foundation Award for Excellence in the Delivery of Social Services. Over three hundred agencies applied for the award. One supporter of the award (a professor who equates public provision of services and progressive taxation with more poverty, homelessness, and family breakdown) noted proudly that all the applicants were "private"—though many received public funds. No-nonsense, "effective" private charities can presumably combine with "the discipline of personal responsibility" to somehow decrease poverty, homelessness, and family breakdown.[21] Although this variant of voluntarism may be difficult to comprehend, it does fall under civil society's umbrella.

A stunning variety of voluntary organizations exist in a country like Canada. Local service clubs like the Lions and the Shriners raise money to assist disabled people and buy new hospital equipment. Heritage conservation groups try to protect old buildings and publish pamphlets on local history. AIDS organizations conduct education and advocacy programs. Other groups deliver hot meals to senior citizens. At the provincial level, groups promote the interests of physicians, farmers, labour unions, and mining companies, particularly in their dealings with government. Others publicize the causes of visually impaired children, Native peoples, and recreational hunters. Nationally, organizations—mostly based in Ottawa—advocate wilderness preservation, promote government funding for the arts, and lobby for approval of bank mergers. Aside from organizations (including some 70,000 registered charities) that have a formal existence, complete with staff, offices, and charitable status, innumerable informal networks of people organize choirs, nature walks, and amateur sports.

In 1997 31.4 per cent of Canadians did regular volunteer work, which adds up to the equivalent of $16 billion in paid work. The voluntarism is highly concentrated, with over 80 per cent of the work donated by about a third of those who volunteer their time.[22] The volunteers serve on boards, provide services from care to coaching, organize events, raise money, and recruit other volunteers. Much of this work is done through places of worship, the part of the voluntary sector that is least dependent on the state.

The rest of Canada's voluntary sector is heavily dependent on government support. This is particularly true of para-public institutions, such as universities and hospitals, which although not formally part of the market are veritable industries employing huge numbers of people in the service sector. But aside from this subsector, other voluntary groups get 49.3 per cent of their revenues from government.[23] Since dramatic reductions in state funding began, the voluntary sector has redoubled its efforts to raise money from the public at large and the private sector. Direct mail campaigns have surged, along with charity bingos, suppertime phone solicitations, and appeals to corporate Canada. Debates over the ethics of accepting money from government-run gambling have preoccupied many volunteer boards. About four out of every five dollars raised by registered charities come from individual donors, who will doubtless continue to be the mainstay of non-governmental support for this sector. Between 1991 and 1995, while state funding cuts deepened, corporate donations dropped from 1.4 per cent of profits to .08 per cent; over half of Canadian corporations with assets over $25 million give no money to charity.[24]

● ● ●

"In our country NGOs and our voluntary sector have become far too dependent on the state," said Al Hatton in a well-received speech to a South Asia Partnership conference on civil society. Hatton is a long-time NGO staff person and leader with many years of experience in Canadian voluntary organization involved in both domestic and international work. He suggested that as a result of government funding the voluntary sector had become overly reactive, "outflanked by the simple and compelling messages of the corporate agenda . . . blindsided by globalization." Even though this sector is pushing for better service and greater participation in a caring society, Hatton said, these "good things" are no longer enough to keep community organizations and NGOs on the public agenda: "This has major repercussions for our independence, our self-reliance, and fundamentally our responsibility to volunteers, members, donors, customers, clients."[25]

The ground is shifting beneath the feet of organizations and movements concerned with what Hatton refers to as "the public good." The basis of this shift, the revival of classical liberalism (Hatton's "corporate agenda"), is an emphasis on the freedom of individuals and corporations to conduct their affairs with minimal interference from the state. Proponents of neo-liberalism advocate less state spending, although the state's role in policing the poor is often intensified, with the welfare bureaucracy becoming ever more invasive as officials harass poor people whose social assistance benefits have already shrunk. Together with traditional conservatives, today's revitalized nineteenth-century liberals often propose a greater role for civil society or the community, NGOs or the voluntary sector, however loosely defined. Government services can be either abandoned completely or left to business or the vaunted voluntary sector. From a different ideological perspective, Jeremy Rifkin argues that this "third sector" offers "the last best hope for re-establishing an alternative institutional framework for a civilization in transition."[26]

What does a sector that "attracts citizens to participate on an unpaid basis as an act of citizenship" really do? Susan Phillips argues that this third sector plays three roles in a country like Canada. It represents people, it engages them, and it delivers services.[27]

• **Representation.** In an era of cynicism about politics and the state, public policy is seen to be more legitimate when the public has been consulted—or has at least appeared to be consulted. The result has been much talk of consulting "stakeholders," which means in turn that the state needs voluntary organizations for legitimation. Ironically, the consultation imperative co-exists with a reduction in state support for citizen participation. (Just as ironically, too, "participation" has come into vogue during a time when authentic participation is becoming more difficult for most citizens.) There was a time when the Canadian state provided significant support for everything from women's organizations to environmental groups, which, it seemed, were less able to find the means of participating than were interests such as Bell Canada or Imperial Oil. So antipoverty groups received funding to represent poor people when the Canadian Radio-television and Telecommunications Commission conducted highly technical regulatory hearings into proposed rate increases by phone companies. A panoply of women's organizations received support to promote a broad feminist agenda. NGOs seeking to raise awareness of global poverty issues among the Canadian public received support from CIDA.

Phillips notes that "representation by groups of citizens is under attack in Canada." Spending cuts have reduced funding for representation. The populist right has targeted what are now derisively labelled as "special interest groups," with the vocabulary easily seeping into the media and the political mainstream. The implication is that only individuals and commercial interests that can afford to conduct formal lobbying have legitimacy. The 1994 hearings of the Special Joint

Committee Reviewing Canadian Foreign Policy were a case in point. Of 561 briefs to the committee, nearly half came from development-oriented NGOs concerned with the aid budget. The tone of the Reform Party's complaint about the hearings could have been lifted from a funding proposal submitted to CIDA by those same NGOs: "Unlike special interest groups . . . grassroots Canadians have a very difficult time participating in such a process."[28] In another context, the Reform Party again differentiated between interest groups and "real Canadians," lamenting how "government programs have crowded out the traditional role of families, communities and local organization in the delivery of personal security."[29]

Spending reductions in the wake of the 1995 federal budget provided a rationale for reducing or eliminating public support for advocacy groups. Ottawa decided that funding priority should go to groups offering direct services. This emerging contract/client relationship between the voluntary sector and the state will lead to a decline in input to the development of public policy. Lobbying by commercial interests continues to receive indirect state support through the tax system because businesses can deduct the direct costs of their own advocacy and lobbying work as well as the fees of the pricey government relations firms they retain. In contrast, according to Paul Leduc Browne: "Voluntary organizations are very often the only voices that can speak to policy makers on behalf of citizens who are less advantaged or privileged. Those with wealth and property are not short of means to let legislators know their views and interests. Workers, people with disabilities, people living in poverty, [and] visible minorities generally do not have comparable advantages."[30]

"Real" or "grassroots" Canadians do remain publicly engaged, but many of them find it increasingly hard to find the time to represent themselves in the complex world of policy development and advocacy. This is particularly true of working people with families, and three-job and four-job families are common in Canada.[31] Citizen engagement through active involvement in political parties—the traditional mode of representation—has collapsed throughout the developed world. Borrowing liberally from the world of marketing and advertising, government hires firms that specialize in doing polls and organizing focus groups. In this way the state takes the pulse of the citizenry without doing so in public.

• **Citizen engagement.** The glue that helps to give people a sense of participation in the life of society, voluntary activity (when freely chosen) can present an attractive contrast to a job of waged work. People get involved in an infinite variety of groups and activities for an almost infinite variety of reasons. Someone who has seen a close relative suffer from a particular disease—or who has herself or himself suffered—may do publicity for the cancer society or raise funds for research into a cure for retinitis pigmentosa. Someone may join the Lions Club as much for fellowship and company as to support the Lions' good works. A woman might chair the board of a child-care centre not because she has young children, but because she once had young children and believes that working women need better child care. A retired professor of botany might conduct nature walks for children because he likes to be outdoors, needs something to do, and believes that promoting environmental consciousness among the very young is an important way of protecting the Earth. People join churches not only because of shared belief systems but also because they cherish organized reciprocity and civic solidarity.

This kind of cultural, non-market activity is important to any society. Good things like trust, responsibility, and diligence comprise what some have termed "social capital"—a factor that often comes up in discussions of civil society in Northern countries. Social capital theorists and some of the more thoughtful representatives of business argue that such activity gives rise to healthier societies and even contributes to economic efficiency. "As we look ahead," says Courtney Pratt, CEO of Noranda, a major Canadian resource company, "social capital is the foundation of economic success in the civil society."[32]

As demographic changes alter the social landscape, voluntary organizations and activity offer Canadians the opportunity to become more socially engaged. More people are taking early retirement in the face of corporate and government restructuring, and with their wide range of skill and experience they are becoming available as potential volunteers. In the years to come the demographic bulge of the baby boom will reach formal retirement age, offering similar opportunities. Increased mechanization means fewer paid workers are needed to produce an ever-greater number of goods and services, and with the computer conquering the service sector the trend will accelerate. On the one hand the resulting productivity dividends could well be privately appropriated, increasing the divisions in an emerging split-level society. On the other hand, Northern countries like Canada could do the creative thing and adopt social policies that encourage—and support—people to work outside the formal waged economy.

• **Service Delivery.** Many formal civil society organizations are concerned with providing some sort of service. These range from Meals on Wheels and helping disabled people remain in their own homes to running food banks or school breakfast programs to feed the increasing numbers of poor children. Although many of the organizations that provide such services have charitable status and are described as voluntary, like the VON they also have employees, large budgets, and complex organizational hierarchies. They are all controlled by volunteer boards. Although formally part of what is called civil society (like virtually all Canadian-based NGOs that sponsor overseas projects) they are also dependent on state funding.

The most efficient, fairest way to deliver services to the public is through a progressive tax system capable of ensuring that citizens support collective goods according to their ability to pay. Those goods include access to decent health care, housing, and education regardless of the individual means to pay for them. This is the system that is now under attack. With the retrenchment of the Canadian state, many of the services once provided on the basis of universality are now falling to the market or to what the interests advocating such changes usually call "the community." Although they exist everywhere, community groups cannot provide universal programs across large regions. Each has a particular focus that reflects the concerns of its founders and the current volunteers and staff. These target constituencies may be well served in some localities, poorly served in others, depending on the whimsical process by which voluntary organizations spring up and sustain themselves.

Increasingly this sector is being identified by the state as the vehicle for delivery of a broad range of public services. Sometimes the services are offered up for tender, with community groups competing against the private sector for contracts. This is what has happened to the Victorian Order of Nurses in Ontario, forced to compete with well-capitalized private-sector care vendors. Sometimes government simply stops supporting people's needs altogether and assumes that the volunteer or third sector will do the job. The result will be an uneven patchwork of service provision, with uncertainty surrounding where the money will come from to support the services. Individual Canadians, already generous in their support of charitable endeavour, are reeling from a deluge of direct mail and phone calls seeking donations. Volunteers put in long shifts in smoky halls, running charity bingos. The private sector has never been a significant supporter of voluntary initiatives; individuals contribute 6.6 times the amount donated by corporations.[33]

Susan Phillips outlines the implications of the looming "contracting regime" for a voluntary sector often praised for its flexibility and local orientation. To secure funding and provide consistent service, organizations are obliged to become more "professional and business-like"—adjectives that have taken on a positive glow.

> More time must be spent on fundraising and more attention devoted to management which often necessitates full-time staff who replace the volunteer accountants or committee members. . . . Service providers may no longer just be serving hot lunches or being big brothers, but working with deeply troubled youth or prison populations. Volunteers may be disinclined to this sort of work or lack the training for it. . . . [American researchers] suggest that the long term impact on the voluntary sector will be that the larger, professional organizations crowd out the smaller ones and that organizations which focus on the needs of the poor are particularly vulnerable because they have greater difficulty attracting private donations.[34]

This does not mean that voluntary or community groups have no role to play in helping the sick or making Canada a better place to live. Indeed, some of the most important innovations in Canadian life in the past thirty years have come from the ground up, to meet the needs of people inadequately served— or entirely ignored—by the welfare state or the market. The child-care system grew out of the feminist movement and the concerns of local women. The network of women's shelters, sexual assault crisis centres, and transition houses now spanning the country emerged from the growing strength of the women's movement. The services provided to women fleeing abusive relationships were initiated not by the state, but by women themselves.

Social movements, though distinct from the formal voluntary sector, constitute a vital aspect of civil society, and recent years have brought an increased recognition of their role. Unlike previous democratic and labour movements, these social movements do not aim to take political power. They do aim to extend both the definition of politics and the scope of political life. The projects of the environmental movement or the efforts by gays and lesbians, indigenous peoples, and disabled people to secure their rights are often clearly political, taking on important advocacy roles. The feminist movement, having struggled to build child-care centres and shelters and much else besides, is obliged to defend its achievements—and that includes gaining state support. But autonomy is crucial for such movements, and few activists would favour the idea of labouring under state control.

Civil society, community initiative, and voluntary organization outside the market are vital underpinnings of political culture. Government responds to the pressures exerted on it by a myriad of social actors, some of them stronger than others. Some have an influence derived from the financial assets at their control. Some have a strength springing from numbers or the power of their argument, from the slow process of winning over and mobilizing lots of people even with few financial resources. The women's movement publicizing the plight of sexual assault victims or pushing for a nationally funded child-care program is an example of civil society acting politically. When a Coalition for Better Childcare pushes for better wages for low-wage child-care workers, it too enters the political arena. When the Canadian Bankers' Association launches a million-dollar lobby campaign to push the government to approve the further concentration of the financial services industry, it is acting politically. Some may regard the CBA (as distinct from its member banks) as a civil society organization. It is certainly a "stakeholder."

Much of what we do, both as individuals and as members of voluntary organizations and social movements, is political in the broadest sense of the term. As such, these activities inevitably involve conflict, an inescapable fact of political life—individual citizens, organizations, classes acting to further their own interests. Although civil society is often described as a third sector distinct from the state and the market, that which is formally public and that which is formally private, it is by no means apolitical. Notions of civil society and community are often sentimentalized, as if they were tranquil meadows of social peace surrounded by the dense, prickly thickets of polit-ical life. This is not the way of the world. Politics permeate all institutions and relationships—anywhere that power relation-ships exist. Social movements change and reconstitute the institutions of civil society. The VON, an organization with fem-inist roots, has been altered both by the evolution of feminism and the growth of the labour movement. At the same time, it remains dependent on the state and is being forced to compete in the market.

In the end, when civil society is affected by politics, it is not simply the politics of elections and parliaments. As Katherine Fierlbeck asks in her discussion of "fetishizing" civil society:

> What does it mean to separate "political" (non-state) society from "civil" society? Must we take this to mean that the myriad groups and organizations within this sphere are not

fraught with their own indigenous form of politics? Most people who have been active participants in any association will probably attest that, no matter how morally earnest the organization is, contestations of power and authority will likely be found not too far underneath the surface. Surely one of the most profound victories of feminist theory in recent decades has been the acceptance of a much broader definition of "power" than that practiced by formal political groups. Power is no longer simply seen as the ability of A to make B do or abstain from an activity but also, less tangibly, the ability to define the political agenda or the ability to shape others' interests with their approval and support. Power suffuses and pervades most instances of social interaction; frequently it is benign and tolerable, but often it is not.[35]

Perhaps it is because so much cynicism and disillusion pervade formal politics in the North—and particularly in North America—that the idea of civil society has contemporary appeal. People are constantly told that there is no alternative to the neo-liberal path, that while it is just fine to have a huge choice at the supermarket, the really important things—well-funded health and education, a clean environment—are now out of reach, beyond the control of citizens or even their elected representatives. They are merely passive spectators at a global game dominated by powerful transnational corporations, though they do get to vote from time to time. Against this background, the idea of a civil society, the proverbial dense network of associations and small groups in which people can actually do something effective, is attractive.

• • •

In 1995 U.S. political scientist Robert Putnam reported to the Trilateral Commission on the state of democracy in the nations of North America, Europe, and Japan. He cited "substantial evidence . . . of mounting public unhappiness with politics and government, discontent deriving in part from real shortfalls in political and government performance." It was not surprising news for the Commission, a think-tank for the Northern corporate elite. Some twenty years earlier the same Commission had heard other academics predict "a bleak future for democratic government."[36]

A sense of anomie, of things falling part, is nowhere more apparent than in the United States, the society that is also the most fertile seedbed for the revival of ideas about civil society. Americans, with their roots in a frontier society of immigrants seeking opportunities and freedoms, have a long tradition of individualism. Although highly patriotic about their homeland, they are suspicious of large government. The French aristocrat de Tocqueville noted that Americans leave society at large to itself. Over a century and a half later, Robert Bellah's team of social analysts observed that their fellow Americans, confronted with dysfunctional public (government, schools) and private (corporate, family) institutions, have remained passive rather than attempting to revitalize them. The result has been a "palpable malaise," a distrust of politics, the loss of meaning in family, a powerless cynicism about business. Bellah and his co-writers say that rather than actively challenging crucial institutions, "American culture has focused relentlessly on the idea that individuals are self-interest maximizers and that private accumulation and private pleasures are the only measurable public goods. We have been blind to the way that institutions enable or cripple our capacity to be the persons we most want to be."[37]

Powerful corporate and state bureaucracies are taken as natural—and unchangeable—features of the landscape, even though long-standing fears of corporate concentration and the inordinate influence of business on government loom ever larger. A job culture threatens to overwhelm family and political culture. The 1996 presidential election saw a record low voter turnout, with almost five million Americans saying that they were too busy to vote or could not take time off work.[38] The 1994 mid-term election that brought a Republican majority to Congress on the promise of a Contract with America (Locke would have been proud) saw fewer than 40 per cent of the electorate bothering to vote. Many remained at home in gated communities, perhaps watching the results on television. Less fortunate Americans, excluded by an electoral system that puts the onus on the individual to register and makes it hard for the poor to do so, shrugged that politics were meaningless to their lives. In *Why Americans Hate Politics*, E.J. Dionne tells his fellow citizens: "We have less and less to do with each other, meaning that we feel few obligations to each other and are less and less inclined to vindicate each other's rights. . . . The abandonment of public life has created a political void that is filled increasingly by the politics of attack and by issues that seem unimportant or contrived."[39]

Anger and negative, scapegoat politics characterize public life in the United States. For some Americans, the solution is to put an end to public provision for the poor, get Tough on Crime, throw more people into jail, and stage speedier executions. In blue-sky California, where university was once accessible to the poorest student because there was no tuition, the costs of higher education are now prohibitive. But ample public funds are still available to support a policy of mass incarceration. California has built twenty new prisons since 1984, with fourteen more planned by 2005.[40]

In papers commissioned by the Trilateral Commission, civil society theorists offer explanations for "massive civic disengagement and social disconnection" and the implications for the future of democracy in the North.[41] Robert Putnam cites the movement of women into the labour force and the rise in working hours of the average American as factors contributing to the decline of civil society in that country. Other factors at play include the "technological transformation of leisure" (read, television-watching), changes in family structure and demographics, and greater geographical mobility. His list does not include politics and market forces.

In the post-industrial vision of the good society, the marketplace is where you make your choices. It's here that the system displays its wonderfully abundant array of products, where people participate by consuming. Freedom is a function of this abundance, and people are free to choose from the market's cornucopia. Milton Friedman, the U.S. economist who is one of the late twentieth century's leading advocates of the neo-liberal path, put the analogy succinctly in a book (*Free to Choose*) co-authored with his wife Rose: "When you vote daily in the supermarket, you get precisely what you voted for and so does everyone else."[42]

Unfortunately, one of the facts of life of the market is that our choices are limited by the resources at our disposal. People anxious about water pollution buy bottled water or purchase purifiers. Those worried about how they will get by in old age use private pensions because they believe the public system will be inadequate. Worries about the quality of public schools spur the growth of private schools. Once we lose faith in public solutions to our problems, the concerns about the lack of social cohesion that propel the civil-society-as-solution also propel individualized, market-based reactions. Market advocates like Friedman ignore a crucial point. The borderless corporate arrangement now styling itself as the market is not the best place for mutual endeavour—or for a flourishing civil society. Nor, indeed, is it the best setting for a healthy political culture, as the U.S. experience shows. In 1990 another U.S. political theorist, Michael Walzer, explained the challenges faced by civil and political society in a globalized world:

> Because the market has no political boundaries, capitalist entrepreneurs . . . evade political control. They need the state but have no loyalty to it; the profit motive brings them into conflict with democratic regulation. So arms merchants sell the latest military technology to foreign powers, and manufacturers move their factories overseas to escape safety codes or minimum wage laws. Multinational corporations stand outside (and to some extent against) every political community. They are known only by their brand names, which, unlike family names and country names, evoke preferences but not affections or solidarities.[43]

In recent discussions of civil society, affections and solidarities are often described as both the glue that helps to bind societies together and the lubricant for democratic life. Some places have better glues and lubricants than others. One of the most thoroughly elaborated arguments in favour of civil society—at least as it exists in the North—has been put forward by Robert Putnam, whose 1993 study *Making Democracy Work: Civic Traditions in Modern Italy* explained that greater levels of reciprocity, trust, and horizontally developed networks of civic engagement in the prosperous Italian north contrasted with the more hierarchical social structures of the south, traditionally viewed as a have-not region. For Putnam, "good government" is associated with membership in "horizontally ordered groups" such as sports clubs, co-operatives, mutual aid societies, and cultural and voluntary associations.[44]

But it was not his research on Italian civic association or work for the Trilateral Commission that thrust Putnam onto the centre stage of American punditry. In 1995 an article by Putnam in the *Journal of Democracy* created a sensation. In the piece, entitled "Bowling Alone"—a reference to his example of the decline of organized league bowling in the United States— Putnam argued that the basis of civil community in the United States had been eroded since the 1960s. Social trust and general reciprocity had gone on the decline, he wrote, as evidenced by the decline of voluntary organizations like the Boy Scouts, the League of Women Voters, and various service clubs. Many scholars, Putnam pointed out, have recognized the importance of vibrant civil society in "the new democracies" of the South and the former Soviet bloc. "To those concerned with the weakness of civil societies in the developing or postcommunist world," he said, "the advanced Western democracies and above all the United States have typically been taken as models to be emulated. There is striking evidence, however, that the vibrancy of American civil society has notably declined over the past several decades."[45]

This argument, backed by the data showing millions of Americans withdrawing from community affairs, caused a considerable stir, especially in the non-profit sector, which was beleaguered by worries about a declining volunteer base. The professor was profiled in *People* magazine and invited to the White House to confer with Bill Clinton, and his thinking influenced that president's State of the Union addresses. The Clinton administration, at the time trying to recover from its 1994 election losses by taking the "values agenda" away from the Republicans, was working to alter the perception of the Democrats as the party of big government. Public hand-wringing about declining trust and reciprocity appealed to those middle-aged Americans who were feeling anxious about not participating in community affairs in the same way that their parents had. Putnam admitted that the decline of local civil society (bowling leagues, Shriners, Masons, and all) had been accompanied by the rise of a few vibrant organizations with huge memberships or support (Oxfam, Greenpeace, and the Sierra Club, for example). But those big NGOs, he argued, lacked an active base. Almost all of their "members" participated by writing a cheque or perusing a newsletter. "Few ever attend any meetings of such organizations," Putnam noted, "and most are unlikely ever (knowingly) to encounter any other member."[46]

He also looked at the role of the labour movement, which has historically done more than just offer citizens the chance to organize themselves to improve both their own wages and working conditions. Politically engaged unions tend to promote universal social programs, and the strength of a country's trade union movement often has a direct bearing on levels of public provision and social inequality. European unions, with their direct political affiliations, are stronger than their U.S. counterparts. During the long boom of the immediate postwar period, U.S. workers were able to bargain for a greater share of the nation's wealth, which helped raise the salaries of non-union employees. By the 1990s all of this had changed. Putnam pointed to the decline in American trade unionism as an important index in the erosion of civil society. "The solidarity of union halls," he lamented, "is now mostly a fading memory of aging men."[47]

But he did not address why or how American unions have been gutted—or to whose benefit. The rise of the service sector and the end of "Fordist" strategies (mass-production runs of standardized goods in large industrial plants like those of car-maker Henry Ford) have given corporations the upper hand, forcing workers' organizations onto the defensive. Changing technologies have facilitated this shift, enabling employers to introduce "flexible specialization" at home and shift production to low-wage regions and countries. Although control over the economy has become ever more concentrated in fewer corporate hands, the operations of these corporations are much more decentralized than in the past. Small workplaces are often more difficult to organize. Contracting out is the order of the day—a massive firm like Nike may not directly employ any workers who actually manufacture shoes. Instead, contractors in Indonesia, India, and Vietnam employ low-wage workers to produce the goods while a "virtual corporation" like Nike organizes the systems and does the marketing across continents.

In this new regime, U.S. workers (along with those in other Northern countries) are told repeatedly that they have to become "flexible." Insecure work arrangements are essentially "subordinated flexibility," because the new flexibility is very much on the employers' terms. The result is not just the increasing income inequality noted by so many observers. It is also the inequality of social class. Flexibility is often about power—who is losing it and to whom. Workers in the United States, Canada, and other Northern countries have lost power to capital. But market ideology is particularly strong in the United States, where in many states unions face overtly pro-business "right to work" laws that make workplace organizing exceedingly difficult.

Ironically, discussions that lament the decline of civil society often ignore these larger phenomena of globalization, of shifting power relations on the job and in society at large. Putnam, for instance, refers to the value of "dense networks of interaction [that] broaden the participants' sense of self, developing the 'I' into the 'we.'"[48] Unions are an important form of civic association, promoting an ethic of service and demonstrating the power of collective action, with members coming together for mutual benefit, although so-called business union-ism can lead to bureaucratization and the decline of demo-cratic structures. But if democracy means people acting togeth-er to shape the decisions that influence their lives, labour can be said to exemplify the democratic spirit.

The civil society argument made by an observer like Putnam tends to paper over political divisions in favour of generalizations that assume all social actors have similar inter-ests. Indeed, idealized civil society organizations often seem to exist in a political and economic vacuum. Some people feel no need to confront large corporations, and there is no recogni-tion of the possibility that widespread discontent with govern-ment is related to an unwillingness to confront that power. Indeed, the Official Story has it that there is no alternative to the power of global business and financial markets, so one might as well get on with localized measures that strengthen voluntarism and support a third sector of civil society organi-zations. Such measures are cheap and can be guided by foun-dation executives and a non-profit sector that promises effi-cient, low-cost service delivery.

As Michael Foley and Bob Edwards put it, writing in the same journal that published Putnam's influential "Bowling Alone" article, certain proponents of civil society, including Putnam, have discounted as "civil associations" any groupings "that advance a cause, pursue policy change as their central vocation, or provoke conflict" even while they say that they want "an activated and engaged populace" and argue "that the socialization performed by civil associations is vital to the creation of an engaged citizenry."[49] Some advocates of civil society clearly don't see any need at all to deal with the thorny questions surrounding the power of capital. They see no need to look to the state and the messy business of politics to ensure the provision of public goods such as health care, education, and decent housing.

If a prominent branch of the civil society debate avoids political questions, politicians have not ignored the matter. Addressing social problems by emphasizing the importance of associational life has an appeal across the political spectrum. The idea of civil society captures the political mood in advanced capitalist countries, where some believe that discontent with existing political arrangements can be effectively addressed by revitalizing bowling clubs and Boy Scout troops. Others feel that free enterprise and fiscal discipline are key to the revival of civil society. Still others, arguing that the history of capitalism offers a legacy of social dislocation, fractured communities, and displaced workers, argue that a "healthy civil society" involves "democratic communities that meet needs for belonging and meaning while struggling against injustice in all spheres."[50] This healthy civil society would have to look at ways of democratizing the state rather than strictly promoting market-based solutions that erode our ability to promote common solutions to common problems.

Another consideration is that the market has always needed to be controlled to prevent social dislocation and fractured communities. This control, this countermovement, is necessary to protect both society—and the free market itself—from the effects of that same, vast, potentially overriding market. Economic and social historian Karl Polanyi, one of the twentieth century's clearest voices on these matters, called the corrosive effects of the market the "disembedding" of the economy from society. The reappearance and dominance of laissez-faire once again reveal this pattern at work. But then again, just possibly, the counterbalance of civil society can work against this disembedding, to fix key social and political elements firmly into place. Just possibly, as writers Jean Cohen and Andrew Arato put it, "The revival of the discourse of civil society reveals that collective actors and sympathetic theorists are still oriented by the utopian ideals of modernity—the ideas of basic rights, liberty, equality, democracy, solidarity, and justice."[51] And just possibly for the practitioners these ideas—these political ideals—will form the essence of any true civil society movement.

# 5

# Dams, Jeeps, and People-Centred Development: **The South Asian Experience**

> Along with popular organizations and NGOs, the use by the funding agencies of 'civil society' reflects a hope, an aspiration. It is believed that somehow traditional elites, corrupt state officials, old-style party bosses and conservative economic forces will wither if 'civil society' is stronger.
> Jenny Pearce, 1997

In May 1998 a group of 150 women and 50 men established "people's checkpoints" (*janata ka naka*) on roads in India's Narmada River Valley, where they had gathered to protest the construction of a large dam. They were soon attacked by police armed with lathis, the long cane that is the crowd dispersal tool of police choice in India. Many of the protestors were beaten, most were arrested, and in the end eighteen truckloads of material made it through to the dam site.

The event was the latest chapter in a lengthy struggle by tribal peoples to protect their sacred Narmada River from the plans of the Gujarat state government, national contractors, and foreign transnationals to build dams that would force them into exile in their own homeland. Originally slated to be one of the biggest in India, the entire Narmada dam scheme would displace 90,000 people from hundreds of villages and from their traditional lands and forests. Earlier in 1998 local people, long used to being ignored by the state government, had won a major victory when an occupation of a dam site combined with an indefinite fast forced a work stoppage pending a complete review of the entire "development" scheme. A full five years earlier they had registered another victory when, combined with a national and international network of supporters, they forced the World Bank—for fifty years the influential institution had spent more money on dams than anything else—to withdraw from funding the full dam project. Still, this success at the international level did not stop the Indian authorities from attempting to implement the project.

In its efforts to protect traditional tribal lands and livelihoods, the international movement against the dams has made use of the latest communications techniques. Within hours of the lathi charge and arrests an e-mail communiqué transmitted around the world by the nine-year-old Narmada Bachao Andolan (NBA, or Save the Narmada Movement) quoted activist Alok Agarwaal: "Eighteen trucks do not a dam make. We know ours is a long struggle and we are determined to fight to the end. Today's action once again confirms that the government is not ready to stand by the genuine demands of the people but will not hesitate to use state-repressive apparatus to favour the national-international capital."[1]

The NBA leadership links resistance to the dams in Central India to other struggles against development plans that threaten to strip the world's most powerless citizens—often indigenous people—of their livelihoods. The campaign against World Bank funding of the Narmada scheme took the NBA's Medha Patkar to Washington, where her contacts with U.S. activists, dramatic testimony to a congressional committee, and meeting with the Bank helped to cut off Bank funding to the project. Joining up with environmental, women's, lower caste, and Gandhian groups, the NBA has been part of the National Alliance of People's Movements, aimed at uniting many of India's myriad popular organizations into "a strong social, political force."[2]

For the NBA, the long fight against the dams was not only about the "destructive development symbolized by large dams" but also an "important symbol of the struggle against the privatization and globalization of the power sector and the economy."[3] Indeed, the international interests that stood to benefit from the construction included several of the largest electrical generation and transmission firms in the world, among them the Swedish/Swiss firm Asea Brown Boveri. In the nineteenth century India's colonial administrators had implemented the Land Acquisition Act, which gave the British the legal grounds for throwing people off their lands. Those rulers would pass the power on to a postcolonial state that continued to deploy it against recalcitrant people who were unwilling to be uprooted.

By 1980 this practice had provoked enough popular resistance that the secretary (irrigation) of the government of India wrote to all state governments, giving official recognition to a state of affairs that was already widely acknowledged: "There has, in recent times, been an awakening on the part of people whose land and property get submerged as a result of the execution of major irrigation, power and multipurpose reservoir projects. It is increasingly being felt that while the forest and tribal areas usually get submerged, the benefits of the projects go largely to the rich farmers."[4]

With this growing opposition in mind, the state of Gujarat had commissioned independent academics to research the "submerging villages" of the Narmada Valley. An exhaustive

102 Civil Society in Question

study described the complex social structure of an area with a highly varied ethnic mix. It also included a brief reference to the activities of several voluntary agencies active in the valley. These included the Rajpipla Social Service Society, run by missionary priests and working "for the cause of social justice and not for the cause of any particular religious denomination." The researchers reported that the RSSS was "well-entrenched" and "very well organized," with roots in the region, providing free legal aid and adult education classes "for the last many years." Another organization was the Yuva Chhatra Sangharsha Vahini (or simply Vahini), made up of "dedicated youths" and part of a national organization started under the inspiration of the late Shri Jayprakash Narayan. The researchers reported that these groups started working on the dam issue in 1980 because they felt the people to be ousted from their land were getting a "raw deal." The report added dryly that local government officials "were not always well disposed towards them."[5]

The period that followed witnessed the growth and consolidation of grassroots opposition to the Narmada Dam and similar developments both in India and around the world. Indigenous people and others facing forced resettlement forged alliances with environmental activists and non-governmental organizations. It would be a mistake, however, to see this as something entirely new, as a sudden flourishing of "civil society." The first mammoth multipurpose dam completed in independent India, Hirakud, provoked stiff opposition, and eventually, in 1946, 30,000 people marching against the project were dispersed by a police lathi charge. In 1970 some 4,000 people occupied the site of the Pong Dam, and eight years later 100,000 demonstrated against the Chandil Dam, with four people killed by police in subsequent protests. In 1983 protestors scored the first major anti-dam victory, forcing the government to abandon the Silent Valley project in Kerala. That project threatened one of the country's few remaining areas of undisturbed rainforest. Popular movements have resisted dam construction from Hungary to Brazil, from Canada to the former Soviet republic of Georgia.

The planning and promotion of dams are most often secretive affairs, carried out behind the closed doors of public and private bureaucracies, remote from the people whose lives will be most affected. The lack of accountability is most obvious in a place like China, where civil society is weak and the "almost incomprehensibly destructive" Three Gorges project threatens to displace some 1.3 million people.[6] Such is the power of the dam-building enterprise that the engineers, financiers, and politicians who support Three Gorges have been relatively free from public scrutiny and control—even though most dams are built with the aid of massive public subsidies. "No difficulty will beat us," boasted Chinese Premier Li Peng, a hydraulic engineer, at the 1995 inauguration of the Three Gorges project.[7]

The industrial hubris of the dam builders reflects a broader sense of domination represented by the projects themselves. The verb most frequently used to describe the dam-building enterprise is "tame." Wild or natural rivers will be tamed by the construction of massive concrete or earth and rock structures. While the costs and risks of this process of domination are public, the benefits accrue to a private few. For the dominators—the developers, the firms, such as Canada's Acres Consulting (which counts Three Gorges and Pakistan's Tarbela in its dam portfolio)—the questions raised by Lewis Mumford's critique of conventional notions of technical progress never do come up: "Are we sure that the control of all natural processes by science and technics is by itself an effective way of relieving and improving man's estate? Is it not possible to have a surfeit of inventions, like a surfeit of food—with similar distress to the organism?"[8]

Such thinking, like that of the tribal people opposed to the Narmada project, goes against the logic of development as it has most commonly been understood in the postcolonial era. Before this era began, the only object that could possibly be conceived of as being subject to underdevelopment was camera film. Critics of development now mark U.S. president Harry Truman's 1949 inaugural address as the starting point in the enterprise, with underdevelopment defined as anything that did not ape the European model of science and industrial progress. "We must embark on a bold new program for making the benefits of our scientific advances and industrial progress available for the improvement and growth of underdeveloped areas," Truman proclaimed.[9] Development was the unalterable course upon which the former colonials had to embark to escape . . . underdevelopment. This was the common sense of the day, and remains so to this day—although it has recently come under attack.

A key source of that attack has been a social movement coalition comprising indigenous peoples as well as development and environmental NGOs: civil society from the ground up—organizations like the Narmada Bachao Andolan, or perhaps more properly the groups that make it up—what Jenny Pearce calls "authentic civil society." But civil society does not always take on this sort of idealized form. India has an intricate tapestry of mass organizations, religious groupings, development organizations, social and co-operative movements, and consumer groups that reflect the crosscurrents and contradictions of a complex society. Some mass organizations are autonomous; others are arms of political parties. Religious organizations perform important welfare functions, though the rise of fundamentalism has caused conflicts within civil society as a whole. Voluntary organizations address poverty issues throughout the country, deploying empowerment strategies but often subject to dependence on either the state or Northern donors. Social movements comprise women, Dalits (untouchables), and people opposed to the ecological destruction wrought by resource development; although they have the potential to group large numbers of people they can also have narrow ethnic or regional bases.[10]

• • •

Writers Lisa Jordan and Peter van Tuijl (associated with the Bank Information Centre in the United States and NOVIB in the Netherlands) argue that democracy has walked tall in the campaign of resistance to the Narmada Dam scheme, a global campaign in which "civil society" crossed over from tribal peoples in the threatened villages to lobby groups in Washington, D.C. From the point of view of the Northern participants, the advocacy work was characterized by a continuous flow of information from North to South and a high level of accountability towards the local people. In their work the tribal peoples, with the assistance of Indian NGOs, focused on government at the state and national levels at home, while international NGOs targeted bilateral aid programs and the World Bank. The campaign invested considerable effort in consultation and mutual understanding, with decision-making shared as widely as possible.

Although resources were shared and people in rural India felt free to make collect calls around the world, with charges paid by the wealthier NGOs, no large flow of funding moved from North to South. In this way the campaign avoided unequal power relations and a situation that could have been more harmful than helpful to the local people. When the people threatened by the Narmada project decided not to co-operate with an outside study of the whole movement, all the international actors abided by their decision. In general, the agenda was "set in close consultation with the groups who [were] supposed to benefit from the campaign and risks [were] assumed only in regards to the burdens that could be borne by the most vulnerable."[11]

Such apparently egalitarian efforts, characteristic of an important (if still thin) strand of today's development enterprise, contrast sharply with earlier missionary or colonial enterprises, in which Westerners ruled morally or militarily, or both. The legacy of colonialism is not restricted to postcolonial laws such as the Land Acquisition Act inherited from the British. It also lingers in ways of seeing and knowing the world: rivers are there to be tamed, nature is there to be dominated, farmers are there to produce cash crops for export. As Edward Said put it, such a vision of the postcolonial world:

> allows the old imperial enterprise full scope to play itself out conventionally, to render the world as official European or Western imperialism saw it, and to consolidate itself after World War Two. Westerners may have physically left their old colonies in Africa and Asia, but they retained them not only as markets but also as locales on the ideological map over which they continued to rule morally and intellectually.[12]

There are numerous struggles against this world view, just as there were against formal colonialism. Many are based in villages and urban slums, part of broad-based social movements pushing to extend democracy beyond the formalities of far-off legislatures, themselves very much part of the colonial inheritance. Such activism attempts to make democracy meaningful to those who have traditionally been excluded—women, workers, land-poor peasants, indigenous people. Some NGOs are attempting to break down the hegemony of hierarchy, redrawing Said's postcolonial "ideological map," so that Southern and Northern groups attempt to work as equals. The struggle to reconstruct global civil society along these lines reflects the Gramscian notion of civil society as a space that has to be revolutionized before radical social change can be contemplated.

The problem, however, is with the very thinness of this egalitarian strand, particularly when one considers the numbers of "civil society" organizations that have sprung up in the postcolonial period. In Nepal, for instance, where NGOs are clearly a growth sector, the number of organizations listed with the government's Social Welfare Council rose from 300 to 6,054 in six short years during the 1990s. There are at least 77 officially registered international NGOs, with unofficial estimates ranging up to 200. There are 15,000 groups registered with the Chief District Administration Offices.[13]

According to the eighth plan of Nepal's National Planning Commission, private and non-governmental organizations could be effective agents of social and economic development in terms of cost, flexibility, motivation, and dynamism. However, according to Nepal's Minister of Local Development, the majority of disadvantaged rural communities (and women in particular) were by 1997 still deprived of their services despite the increased NGO presence in the country. The minister reported that NGOs were concentrated at the centre and, instead of being self-reliant, were becoming more dependent on foreign assistance.[14]

But, although NGO-based aid is relatively new to Nepal, civil society is not. As a multi-ethnic nation, Nepal is home to a tremendous variety of traditional associations and indigenous groups concerned about everything from credit and savings initiatives to resource management, entertainment, education, and cultural preservation. These are not necessarily initiatives that participants have conceived of as "development" in the formal, Northern sense, but they have continued in parallel fashion alongside the modernized, NGO version of civil society that has emerged as part of the development enterprise.

According to Nanda Shrestha, who grew up in the central Nepalese town of Pokhara in the 1950s, the notion of development only really began to gain currency in his homeland during that decade. Since the word for it was *bikas*, a division emerged between modernized people identified as *bikasis* and those more traditional folk who were *abikasis*. Shrestha recalls that in those days *bikas* "looked glistening and sumptuous"— formal education, consumer goods, jeeps (and roads), English, airplanes (and airports), electricity (and dams). Modern, educated *bikasis* were different than their fellow citizens, so that *bikas* gained a distinct class character that magnified the class biases of colonial society.

Shrestha believes that *bikas* and the foreign aid that was so important in achieving it eroded self-reliance while doing little to reduce poverty and hunger. *Bikas* disrupted older patterns of social organization. If a trail got washed out or otherwise damaged, people from surrounding villages who had previously organized themselves for the necessary repairs began turning to "somebody else, a foreign donor or a government agency," he says. "Nowadays nothing moves without foreign aid." What's more, with the introduction of consumerism, poverty changed character, becoming more frightening and degrading. "Prevailing modes of life were vilified by development fetishism acquired from the West."

A new form of materialism seeped into the indigenous culture and society. Like many critics of modernity-as-development, Shrestha is at pains to distance himself from the ideal of some Arcadian past, the romantic notion that whatever was old was good, that the old social structure should be revived. But he argues: "The indigenous economic system and values were generally self-reliant, self-sufficient, sustainable and far less destructive of humanity as well as nature. . . . We learned to seize the currents of international development, propelled by the World Bank, the US Agency for International Development. . . . We turned their fads into overriding national concerns, instantly churning our reports to corroborate our claims." For this expatriate (Shrestha eventually found himself teaching business at a university in Florida, thanks to contacts with U.S. aid workers), the jeep was the symbol of *bikas*: "second-hand and out of reach of the masses."[15]

Rohit Kumar Nepali of SAP Nepal echoes Shrestha's anxiety about the Nepalese experience. He reports that NGOs in his country tend to be overcentralized in the capital and dominated by high-caste people, with neither the government nor many NGOs or large donors initiating projects in support of indigenous or popularly based NGOs. But the sector has continued to grow in light of the "market and state failure in meeting the basic needs of the majority." Nepali sees two tendencies at work among NGOs. Along with the state, some NGOs have submitted themselves to the market and large donors like the World Bank to complete the "global process of homogenization of consumer culture," which compels villagers "to come under the roof of [the] global village." According to Nepali, "Both governmental and non-governmental organizations have intensified their activities in the villages through induced people/community-based organizations in order to make villagers dependent on [multinational corporations] to satisfy falsely generated needs."[16]

The technique here is to use "induced people/community-based organizations" to increase dependency on markets. This tendency is backed by the recipe for manic modernization recommended by the World Bank, the familiar blend of externally oriented development (dams, forestry, and tourist infrastructure in the Nepalese variant) coupled with privatization, cuts in subsidies for essential goods and services, and deregulation. Nepal's 1995-96 budget advocated the abolition of wealth taxes and the introduction of a regressive value-added tax, while in the following year the Congress-led coalition backed subsidy cuts to public utilities and power privatization. In a country in which 60 per cent of the people live in poverty, ample funds are available for luxury hotel developments. The mountain air is polluted with uncontrolled vehicle emissions. The Kathmandu Valley has 100,000 vehicles on the road every day, with lead levels in the capital hitting 500-700 parts per million—1,000 times higher than the safe standard. In a countryside increasingly denuded of forest cover, villagers who can no longer find wood turn to cattle dung for fuel, thereby reducing the soil fertility. The country has neither regulatory agencies nor environmental legislation.[17]

Nepali contrasts this tendency with the second, which reflects the need to support indigenous organizations in the struggle for local self-rule and autonomy. He points to increased activism and understanding of "people-centred development" along with a growing awareness of the importance of self-help and community-based organizations. A momentum for change (although in a "very rudimentary form") has begun to be established at a local level, albeit with significant caveats. No common collective platform exists for people to raise their concerns, and people are still fighting the battle against poverty in isolation.[18]

This conclusion is borne out in the case of the successful national and international effort to put a halt to the Arun Dam project, a U.S.$764 million scheme to produce hydro power for urban and export markets from the remote Arun Valley. The plan provoked resistance in Nepal and mobilized the international anti-dam movement, coinciding with the World Bank's Inspection Panel. Two Nepalese NGO coalitions (the Alliance for Energy and the Arun Concerned Group) played a key role in the campaign, which resulted in the World Bank's withdrawal from and the resulting termination of the project. But unlike the Narmada opposition movement, the forces opposing the dam and the local people forged few solid links. As a result, when the Bank announced it would not back the project, Nepalese NGOs were reluctant to declare a major victory for fear of generating a backlash from local interests that would have benefited from the project—while international NGOs "were releasing a statement which presumed that Nepalese people were dancing in the street."[19]

People-centred development (perhaps a different form of *bikas*) along with decentralized efforts that would give voice to powerless people in local areas—as proposed by Rohit Kumar Nepali—would have resulted in a campaign involving the people whose lives would have been most affected, enhancing their capacity not only to oppose outside initiatives but also to strengthen existing forms of civil society.

*Bikas* can mean more than jeeps and dams. Development really can spring from the self-generating notion of *se développer*. The French verb is often reflexive—to "develop oneself." But this is very difficult to achieve, particularly from outside. Activists interested in promoting these good things can move in this direction when they search out the already existing networks that local peoples use to survive. Indigenous, often ingenious, forms of production and exchange sustain people through good times and bad. Understanding and working with

those structures are crucial if words like empowerment, participation, and capacity-building are to have real meaning. People
are always participating in the construction of their own history. They have the capacity to provide collective goods at the
local and regional levels. In the South the state may sometimes
be strong, and hasty, in dealing with dissident movements, but
it is often weak in the face of international capital (and multilateral agencies) and incapable of providing public goods, such
as health, education, and environmental protection. Such services are among the collective goods that people must provide
for themselves through traditional forms of mutual aid. As
David Sogge puts it:

> Poor people, like everyone, prefer to rely, where they can,
> on means they can control. That usually comes down to
> relying on their own devices. They survive chiefly through
> the shrewd use of local circuits of goods, services and
> migrant labour. Here and there, a flow of benefits from a
> foreign aid programme may fit into a survival strategy for
> awhile. But Africans, Asians and Latin Americans organize
> their own richer-to-poorer flows with great efficiency. . . .
> Much of the aid industry carries on in complete ignorance
> of such huge but unregistered systems of self-help.[20]

What Sogge is describing is informal, everyday civil society. It
happens when people from a remote village get jobs in a city
and send part of their earnings home, sharing whatever
prosperity they have with their kin. It also unfolds globally,
when circumstances at home in Nepal (or Pakistan or the
Philippines or Guatemala) force poor people to migrate to the
North. And it is a way of life in many Southern societies where
market relations have not colonized traditional forms of barter,
exchange, and mutual aid. Although often unrecognized,
embedded in tribal, religious, or caste structures, and only

partially effective in meeting people's basic needs, these systems still have their own considerable capacities. Such structures are rarely concerned with stopping internationally financed megaprojects; they more often limit themselves to modest goals that they have the capacity to achieve. NGOs and activists can assist in enhancing that capacity when they establish roots in local soil. This is not an easy task, particularly when NGOs are staffed by people from class or ethnic backgrounds different from those of the people at the grassroots—the people whose efforts (at participation, empowerment) they hope to assist.

● ● ●

In Pakistan the number of formal NGOs rose from a few hundred in the early 1980s to over ten thousand in the 1990s. According to SAP Pakistan, NGOs and civil society organizations are limited by "isolation from each other and the overall social and political movements." They are also narrowly focused on a "traditional welfare approach to development," and their achievements are limited. Moreover, they tend to comprise more modernized elements of the population that may have a welfare approach to development and do not always have close links to poor communities: "Most organizations are set up by individuals who are relatively better-off in socio-economic terms, better educated and wield a certain amount of influence. Their total control of the organization at one level results in outputs and on the other has the tendency to make the communities/beneficiaries dependent."[21]

SAP Pakistan recognizes the significance of a problem that, along with the fragmentation of civil society, limits the effectiveness of such organizations. There is also the issue of supply creating demand: some organizations have sprung up because donors and large NGO support groups need recipients for their programs. SAP has attempted to address such problems by playing the role of catalyst, enhancing the capacity of NGOs, trade unions, peasant organizations, and women's groups as well as civil liberties and advocacy organizations.[22]

Modern civil liberties groups gained prominence in Pakistan in response to the repression of Muhammad Zia ul-Haq's martial law regime (1977-88). Similarly, feminism came up against traditional Islamist conceptions of the role of women in society. Modern proponents of popular empowerment, reacting against the stringent strictures of state and patriarchy, seek to support the NGO version of civil society. For some this includes a hopeful vision of democracy: people establishing, with their own hands, the conditions of their own freedom.

But civil society in a country like Pakistan—and in any country, for that matter—is not uniform. It is fraught with crosscurrents and contradictions. It reflects political divisions. Mohammad Qadeer argues that civil society in Pakistan has been crucial in bringing about the end of entire political regimes, including the governments of Mohammah Ayub Khan (1958-69) and Zulfikar Bhutto (1971-77).

During Ayub Khan's time in power, according to Qadeer, new forms of civil society "evolved from a relatively cohesive clan-based social organization into social formations based on ethnicity and class interests, as well as primordial ties." During Bhutto's rule civil society's centre of gravity shifted towards what Qadeer calls "primordial," or fundamentalist, groups. The mosque became a centre for social mobilization, with clerics, landlords, traders, and informal sector *bazaaris* gaining influence while urban professionals, commercial and industrial interests, and organized urban labour saw their fortunes decline. The traditionalists, with their base in the conservative fragment of civil society, helped to bring Bhutto down and pave the way for General Zia ul-Haq's suffocating regime. While human rights and feminist organizations solidified themselves and resisted, the military in coalition with the traditionalists held sway. The press and the judiciary were stifled. Migration from country to city and emigration from Pakistan accelerated, and remittances from workers who migrated to the Persian Gulf provided a key prop to the economy and many families. (This is one of the many ways people outside NGO and aid circuits devise their own coping strategies.)

"Democracy," observes Iftikhar Malik, "was portrayed as an anathema to Islam."[23] According to Mohammad Qadeer: "The Islamic faction in civil society gained at the cost of secular, modern and urban interests. This reordering of civil society helped sustain the Zia regime for 11 years. . . . The cumulative result of Zia's policies has been the division of Pakistani society into sectarian, ethnic and ideological fragments. These primordial social organizations were not new, but they have gradually come to dominate civil society."[24]

The other "track" of civil society, represented by human rights organizations, NGOs, and groups concerned with social justice, is active and far from moribund. Qadeer argues, however, that their roots are not as deep as their more traditional rivals, and their capacity to mobilize mass support is more limited. The paradox here is in their relation to the state. Most formal, modern organizations need a responsive state, enforceable law, and a capable public sector if they want their demands for social justice and human rights to have any real traction.

When the state is instable (Pakistan had nineteen prime ministers and twenty-four years of military rule in the years from independence in 1947 to the mid-1990s), weak, or corrupt, the organizations have only a limited effectiveness. Many NGOs still act as informal social service agencies, often with the assistance of foreign aid agencies for which they undertake contracts. When a weak state has difficulty providing public goods on anything approaching a universal scale, denominational organizations with broader social bases can often fill the gap to a greater or lesser degree. Such forms of civil society cannot, however, protect the environment from being degraded or resources from being overexploited. Nor can they adequately meet urgent needs for a fair body of law, urban education and health services, a safe water supply, and sewage services. Countries in which the state is corrupt or inefficient or both, with civil society weak or divided, will have grave difficulties promoting and protecting the delivery of collective goods.

This is not to say that denominational charity groups, NGOs, or civil society itself cannot administer sufficient programs to help furnish excluded people with basic needs. The residents of a poor community can come together to build a school or a clinic with materials supplied by charity. Families can donate funds to support relatives in need. Whole communities can benefit when young people who have migrated to the city or some foreign metropolis send money home. Such mutual aid occurs everywhere. It is necessary, but it is seldom or never enough. Without state programs and policies that allow schools and hospitals to function with adequate supplies, equipment, and staff, civil society—no matter what its orientation—will continue to fight a rearguard action against inequality and exclusion. And without a vibrant civil society pushing for collective goods and adequate standards, the state will most likely neglect public welfare while representing or responding to powerful groups, like the military establishment, a landowning elite, or a wealthy business class.

A Mexican sociologist, Carlos M. Vilas, argues that while social movements grounded in civil society can effectively deal with particular aspects of a social problem, getting at the structural causes of poverty is another matter. "This depends on global state policies regarding employment, income and welfare, whose designs are usually beyond the reach of social movements," he says. Ignoring structural issues (such as neoliberal structural adjustment policies and international trade treaties) and concentrating on identities (such as ethnic nationalism and other fundamentalisms) are dead-end streets. Civil society and social movements "must figure out how to articulate their demands within the political system." When social movements activate civil society, the concept of citizenship can be broadened "to include a social dimension."[25] Forging new kinds of links with political parties can be part of this. Both representative democracy and popular control over social decisions—the matters that have an impact on people's daily lives—must carry across both spheres: political and civil society.

Activists concerned with social justice find themselves straddling this fine line between civil and political societies. Certainly, civil society in any country—whether informal, village-based self-help initiatives or NGOs and social movements—would not seem to be capable of dealing by itself with the World Trade Organization or corporations like Asea Brown Boveri. Civil society by definition must work within the confines of the state, both the totalitarian and militarized variant and the more benign, democratic form.

● ● ●

In 1991, when the Ranasinghe Premadasa regime in Sri Lanka appointed a commission to look into NGO activities, the focus was on the large Sarvodaya organization as well as the political role played by NGOs and civil society in general. The commission, reflecting the regime's authoritarian nationalism, deemed civil society to be basically a Western concept, observing that some NGOs had "transgressed their proper limitations."[26]

The long United National Party (UNP) rule—beginning in 1977 and ending in 1993 with Premadasa's assassination—had initially brought to an end one of the South's more advanced welfare states and thereafter saw the introduction of the usual liberalization measures, including privatization, removal of subsidies for fertilizers and other goods, deregulation of the tariff system, and cuts to the public sector. Those years were also marked by civil war and the demise of liberal democracy. By 1992 the World Bank's *World Development Report* was revealing income disparities in Sri Lanka surpassed only by Brazil, one of the most notoriously divided countries in the world. According to a 1992 report by the International Fund for Agricultural Development, from 1965 to 1988 Sri Lanka experienced the most dramatic increase in rural poverty among the 114 countries studied.

Not surprisingly, a number of NGOs had emerged and were attempting to provide welfare services that had previously been the preserve of the state. The beleaguered Sarvodaya, with its emphasis on self-help, had long been the largest NGO in the country but was now joined by a host of others. Foreign funds became available, and numerous groups committed to human rights, democracy, and ethnic reconciliation took root, from the Movement for Inter-racial Justice and Equality to Women for Peace, from the Civil Rights Movement to People's Action for Free and Fair Elections. Their names evoked goals not apparently shared by the regime. A report by the International Commission of Jurists, issued in 1991, soon after the formation of the government commission on NGOs, described a "palpable fear of impending—and even of actu-al—victimization by the government" within the NGO commu-nity.[27] There were suspicions that the government had little interest in regulating NGOs and was, rather, attempting to intimidate them.

According to Paikiasothy Saravanamuttu, a Sri Lankan academic and columnist, while the opposition party "lay large-ly dormant" during the UNP regime, civil society groups "mounted resistance and voiced criticism against authoritari-anism." Saravanamuttu points out that activist organizations worked both directly and indirectly to put the opposition People's Alliance coalition into office when the UNP regime finally came to an end, with some leading critics even framing the election manifesto.[28] Evidently the UNP government's con-cerns about the nature of at least part of Sri Lankan civil soci-ety were well founded. The fine line between civil and political society becomes even finer when people active in civil society organizations become involved in politically partisan activities.

No government, in any society, can ever enjoy untroubled relationships with groups in civil society. The interests of the state rarely coincide with those of the myriad of organiza-tions—social movements, religious groups, community devel-opment organizations, cultural and professional associations, the list is almost endless—that make up civil society. The state's usual impulse is to try to channel and control civil initia-tives according to its own ideological leanings. Groups in civil society have their own axes to grind, often in opposition to prevailing state policy.

When that relatively new factor—the NGO—is inserted into the civil society equation, matters get more complex. In Sri Lanka the World Bank began investing heavily in programs to offset the negative effects of the structural adjustment policies it promoted there. "The Bank realizes that even if its clients' economies responded well," wrote a former U.K. agency head who also worked for the Bank in Sri Lanka, "a large segment of the population . . . would not benefit."[29] During the UNP rule, in an attempt to dull the edge of the egregious inequality and poverty that resulted, the Bank led an interagency group that allocated $87.5 million to a new National Development Trust that quickly became a political tool of the government. A key player in the regime was installed as chair of the Trust, which was quickly renamed the Janasaviya Trust Fund (JTF), causing confusion among citizens who had been exposed to ample publicity about the UNP's own antipoverty program, which was conveniently called Janasaviya. Key staff were recruited from the civil service and state-owned banks. So the Bank initially failed to create an NGO-based program insulated from politics.

After the demise of the UNP regime in 1993, the JTF was able to begin directing money to an NGO sector that expanded rapidly in response to the new supply of cash. New NGOs emerged, and the JTF developed, in the words of the World Bank official, "a portfolio of partners that range from excellent to poor." Some of these sprang up in response to the existence of the new donor. Several of the new "partners" were headed up by people who had gained management experience in the huge Sarvodaya NGO. According to Roland Hodson, "The normal market forces of supply and demand apply even to the provision of services in the NGO sector."[30]

Outside forces can influence the normal tension between state and civil society. The attention being paid to civil society in donor circles had led the Sri Lankan (UNP) government to initiate a move to "establish" a civil society that included a forum for NGOs. Saravanamuttu points out that this sudden interest most likely sprang from the existence of Norwegian programming in this area.

> The invitation from the Ministry (of Ethnic Affairs and
> National Integration) to join the government in "establishing
> civil society" . . . is indicative either of the ignorance of the
> ministry on the process of civil society building, or of an
> attempt to co-opt civil society groups to fulfil its mandate. . . .
> The ministry official chairing the discussion appeared to
> operate on the assumption that the NGO groups represented
> were primarily interested in the funds that the ministry would
> be able to disburse.[31]

Given the experience of watching NGOs spring up in response
to a supply of funding (from the World Bank, Northern NGOs,
or wherever) it is hardly surprising that government officials
would view "civil society" as something that can be established
at the stroke of a pen, the purchase of letterhead, or the manufacture of a mission statement. Though this might strike political theorists as odd, it rings true to the former civil servants
and other canny job-seekers who are on the ground in countries like Sri Lanka.

The extent and activity of NGOs, as one of many manifestations of civil society, are influenced by changes in the nature of
the state and the market. In South Asia, with the recent legacy
of authoritarian rule, shifts in the nature of the state have been
particularly noteworthy. In the Sri Lankan case, the NGO sector expanded with the erosion of the welfare state, the need to
check the excesses of a heavy-handed government, and the
new supply of funding.

• • •

Bangladesh is a poorer country than Sri Lanka. For instance,
one of the economic-social indicators, adult literacy, is at 90
per cent in Sri Lanka, while in Bangladesh it is at 37 per cent.

Bangladesh has a different political culture and a huge number of NGOs. But before the rise of the NGO, the country witnessed an increase in popular movements that undertook political action without recourse to the formal politics of the ballot box. In the 1950s, well before the break with Pakistan, a major peasant uprising emerged to protest the outrages of a share-cropping arrangement under which landless farmers provided all the labour and other inputs in agricultural production only to gain a mere third of the crops they produced. Some two-thirds of the produce went to the powerful landlord class. The Three-Division Movement took on this unjust system, mobilizing peasants and provoking violence, to which the state responded in kind. In the end the peasants emerged with half a share of the wealth they produced.

The Three-Division Movement may or may not be an example of civil society in action. What is clear is that in a rural society with some two-thirds of the population engaged in agriculture, semi-feudal land-tenure arrangements persist. Landlessness is endemic. Fewer than 10 per cent of the country's rural households own over half of the arable land, while a third of the families own no land at all. If one includes households that own less than half an acre, 62 per cent of the families in rural Bangladesh are functionally landless.[32] This inequality is reflected in conflicts over the growing impact of shrimp cultivation in Bangladesh, where from the mid-1980s to the mid-1990s over a hundred people were killed in land disputes over shrimp aquaculture.[33] Although the Bangladeshi lose ten agricultural jobs for every job created in aquaculture, the World Bank and other multilateral agencies in co-operation with the state have promoted shrimp as a key Bangladeshi export commodity. Intensive shrimp farming has resulted in that product becoming the country's third-largest export.

This production has been accomplished at the expense of ecological diversity and a traditional shrimp fishery that long co-existed with rice cultivation. In general, the phenomenal expansion of the global shrimp business is a telling example of the priorities of those who attempt to manage the world economy while simultaneously prescribing what's good for the poor. It is a world in which one-fifth of the people consume four-fifths of the resources. Consumption of shrimp in wealthy countries (United States, Japan, and Western Europe) jumped by 300 per cent from 1987 to 1997, but the price of shrimp plummeted from U.S.$14 a pound in 1986 to $5 in 1996—while all the time multilateral development banks were pushing poor countries to devote more effort to exporting shrimp that only a tiny minority of their people could ever afford to eat.[34]

In Bangladesh land flooded with saline water for industrial shrimp production no longer supports local needs for livestock, fuel wood, milk, and dung for fuel. Armed guards surround flooded land that produces tiger shrimp for luxury markets abroad, an ironic development for a country that imports basic food grains to support even the low calorie intake of its people. In this country, according to one NGO director, "to be poor is to own nothing, not even the land on which one's bamboo house is built, and to feel fortunate to eat one plate of rice in a day."[35]

Coastal people have initiated mass protests, sparking widespread resistance to the transformation of the local environment and indigenous economy for the benefit of outside industrial landowners. Their efforts have been supported by organizations like Nijera Kori, an NGO that works with landless people in Bangladesh, and the policy research group UBINIG, which has helped the fisher community of Badarkhali initiate Nayakrishi Andolan (the New Agriculture Movement) to promote local varieties of vegetables and rice, chemical-free multi-cropping, and seed conservation by a community seed bank.

It would seem that the presence of a vibrant civil society active in mobilizing people hurt by development schemes can only be beneficial. The level of local and international mobilization has not approached that of the tribal people threatened by the Narmada Dam in India. But popular organizations along the Indian coast have fashioned a People's Alliance Against the Shrimp Industry to co-ordinate opposition to aquaculture and to organize and lobby internationally. Out of these efforts has come the International Network Against Unsustainable Aquaculture, which organized a mock trial of shrimp aquaculture, documenting the destructive impact of the industry and presenting an NGO position to the United Nations. NGOs in Bangladesh have also joined other elements of civil society in big-P politics, campaigning for free and fair elections, conducting voter education campaigns, and helping to ensure that women participate in the electoral process.[36]

Those efforts are tiny compared to the huge NGOs that have appeared in Bangladesh since the country was formed. The Grameen Bank, BRAC (the Bangladesh Rural Advancement Committee), and Proshika are the best-known. Thousands more exist, to the extent that many NGOs suffer from staff shortages and some organizations poach experienced workers from others. According to Philip Biswas, director of the Rural Reconstruction Center, a Bangladeshi NGO, certain districts possess dense networks of NGOs, which overlap and compete for clients, while other areas have few if any active NGOs. Moreover, large NGOs often move in on territories where smaller groups are already working, resulting in a duplication of work.[37]

Yet Grameen and BRAC do have impressive programs that

provide poor people with crucial credit, education, and health services. BRAC delivers education more efficiently and at lower cost than the state. Like Sri Lanka's Sarvodaya, BRAC has become a major national institution, complete with a large staff, an impressive headquarters building, and its own printing press. But unlike its Sri Lankan opposite number, BRAC's smooth operations extend to its relations with consortia of foreign donors. Its experiences have not been as troubled as Sarvodaya's. Which is not to say that the enterprise has not had its critics. BRAC's highly regarded network of primary schools has been attacked by Islamic fundamentalists who do not appreciate equal education for girls and boys and other forms of creeping modernity. Like many other externally funded NGOs, BRAC is always open to the charges of outside interference. It has had to deal with its schools being burned and the unfounded charge that it is a covert scheme to Christianize children.

From another perspective comes the criticism that large-scale NGOs like BRAC do not increase the capacity of the poor to organize independently to challenge structural inequalities and stand up to powerful interests like landlords. This critique points to the role played by some organizations in rolling back the state. Granted, the state is often corrupt and inefficient. But, argue David Hulme and Michael Edwards:

> What is unclear is whether this rolling back has strengthened the role of communities as citizens to influence state actions, as is commonly assumed by those who view BNGOs as based exclusively in civil society; or whether it has contributed more to the identification of the private sector as the main provider of essential goods and services for the entire population (including the poor and disadvantaged). This latter position views the poor as consumers whose needs can be most efficiently met by the private sector.

NGOs are analyzed as non-profit private agencies accountable through the forces of competition in an open market.
Beneficiaries and members become "customers" (as BRAC in
Bangladesh now terms the poor) and claims to be strengthening civil society become redundant.[38]

Political interventions involve active, complex, difficult organizing. The struggle against the depletion of fish stocks off the
Kanyakumari district of the state of Tamil Nadu in Southern
India is a case in point. The combination of globalization of
demand, incursions by factory ships, technological change in
the local fishing industry, and general overfishing has produced a volatile situation. The government of India has
licensed foreign factory ships at the same time as trawler
fishers and some small boats have adopted motorized equipment. Trawlers owned by local merchants employ fishers and
compete with family-based artisanal fishers. Women who once
made nets from local cotton have lost that work in the face of
machine-made nylon nets, so they have organized co-operatives to market fish locally.

Many of the people involved on all sides of this issue come
from the same communities. Organizing efforts aimed at resisting the incursions of factory ships that operate on the other
side of the horizon (but with the same ecosystem) are made
more difficult by intense conflicts that often erupt between
local people. Attempts to agree on a division of the small-scale
fishery between small crafts and trawlers have often broken
down. Tension within communities persists, occasionally flar-
ing into violence.

The often seamless vocabulary of "community" that
pervades much talk of civil society tends to neglect the very
real fractures in the social architecture of particular locales,
some long-standing, some wrought by recent changes.

Although collective action against the depletion of the fishery in Tamil Nadu has involved road blockages, fasts, delegations to government offices, and links with national networks opposed to foreign mega-trawlers, activists also report that the presence of television in villages makes it difficult to hold meetings during a time slot when popular soap operas are broadcast. Partisan party politics, in which some of Tamil Nadu's famous film stars are deeply involved, are an important factor in the Kanyakumari district. The issue of the state's relationship with the rest of the country is ever-present. Modern forms of wage labour—jobs with the local merchant class that owns trawlers, and migration to the Persian Gulf—have made communities more complex. The expansion of formal education has divided the youth of fishing communities between boys who stay in school and those who apprentice in the artisanal fishery. Technological change (motors, nets, the general increase in scale of the fishery) has dramatically altered the local industry, as has the competition from foreign trawlers.

Despite local conflicts and difficulties in co-ordinating with national groups, local activism successfully linked with larger networks to oppose the Indian government's plans to license mega-trawlers that would threaten the marine ecology. The efforts culminated in a 1996 mobilization and one-day strike that resulted in policy changes that favoured local fishers. People can organize across the divisions of interest and class that characterize civil society, even when broader changes are making their societies more complex.[39]

People's adaptations to changing conditions carry implications for organizing. How NGOs—local, national, donor—take the complexity of civil society into account will be crucial. They will have to consider how market forces are shaping class, ethnic, and gender relations, how people are reacting to integration into the global economy. They will have to contemplate the appeal of long-standing nationalisms in the age of globalization. State policies will influence that integration. NGOs will have to monitor, take into account, the responsiveness (or lack of same) of party politicians and governments to demands for open markets or to questions of democracy and accountability. They will have to watch out for certain signs: whether, for instance, the state is strong when dealing with popular demands for accountability from fishers or peasants displaced by shrimp farming, but weak in the face of pressures from investors, landlords, or multilateral agencies.

The societies of South Asia are older and easily as complex as the places in which industrialization first prompted thinkers from Adam Ferguson to Antonio Gramsci to write (in very different ways) about civil society. Some precolonial societies were more democratic than others. This is particularly true when democracy is defined as the urge of people to create, by themselves, a situation in which they control the forces that have an impact on their daily lives. These include economic *and* political forces. A truly democratic vision involves democratizing both the state and the market.

This is no easy task given that democracy often depends on the painstakingly slow process of building up local organizations, and that this must be done during an era in which the economy is being increasingly internationalized by forces unaccountable to anyone but themselves. This is why, as the Czech Republic's president Václav Havel put it to the U.S. Congress in 1990, democracy will always be an ideal that can never be fully attained. Some governments remain more democratic and accountable than others, and authoritarian regimes, like great empires, do wane. Meanwhile, those parts of civil society genuinely interested in achieving goals of political and economic advancement, of social justice, do not simply contend for a measure of control over prevailing political practices and institutions. They also do the slow, difficult work of organizing to empower themselves.

# 6

# Conclusion: **Towards the "Double Movement"**

The swish of plaid kilts, the skirl of the pipes: these are the symbols of an idealized Scotland. Not Glasgow's gritty housing estates, not the electronics plants that dot the Lowlands, but the romantic Highland lochs and glens that beckon visitors with barren beauty and obscure malt whiskies.

Tartan and the pipes have not always been symbols employed to attract tourists. Two and a half centuries ago they were banned by the English authorities as symbols of Jacobite rebellion. The Crown saw the Scottish nationalism that it had defeated at the Battle of Culloden in 1746 as a poisonous form of treason and a threat to its existence. The Hanoverian regime under King George II had some reason for anxiety, for the Jacobite troops under "Bonnie Prince Charlie" had abandoned their march on London only 127 miles north of the city. The English rulers knew that the French saw Scotland as a second front in their wars against the English, and scare stories about French landings on the Channel coast swept London regularly. The Scottish advance into England was bankrolled both as a venture capital scheme by a Paris banking house and from money borrowed against Prince Charlie's mother's jewels. The much-romanticized Charlie fled, leaving his followers to face the gallows, the prison scows, or forced transportation to King George's American colonies.

One of the results of the defeat of the rebellion was the radical dismantling of Highland society that unfolded over the next century. The Highlands were cleared of trees and people. The Gaelic-speaking clans defeated at Culloden comprised a traditional society still rooted in a time far different than the supposedly modern, commercial-industrial era emerging in England and the Scottish Lowlands during the late eighteenth and nineteenth centuries. Popular historian John Prebble describes the story of what happened to the Highlanders, "the ordinary men and women who were involved in the last Jacobite Rising," as part of "a sickness from which Scotland, and the Highlands in particular, never recovered."[1]

"After 1746," notes a more scholarly observer, "the ancient *Gemeinschaft* of pre-civil society disappeared altogether, leaving the way clear for Hanoverian progress, agricultural enclosure or clearance, and the development of trade and industry."[2]

In the aftermath of defeat and in the course of the "modernization" of their land, many Scots had to leave a country that no longer seemed to offer promise. The period 1756-1815 saw between 40,000 and 75,000 Highlanders recruited into the British army. Landowners received cash grants if they became recruiting sergeants. After losing their principal colony to republican elements in America, the British saw one of the principal tasks of their expanding Imperial army to be the pacification of India, the newest jewel in the Crown of Empire. Although tartan and the pipes were banned in Scotland, they could readily be seen on dusty tracks and city streets from the Punjab to Calcutta, where the British colonial authorities, deeming it wise to encourage loyalty, allowed their Highland regiments to maintain their traditions. Administration followed the flag, and Scots made up the most prominent element in Britain's colonial regime in India.[3] The commercial order introduced in Scotland was gaining a foothold in South Asia, with similar consequences for native life.

● ● ●

At first glance this historical snippet may appear to have little to do with civil society and the promise it holds (or may not hold) for democracy or economic efficiency or social justice. But like any story involving political power and changing ways of organizing the world, it can tell us something about how notions of progress and development differ according to where people sit—whether they are on the bridge of the ship or down in steerage. And it also bears on the idea of civil society because Adam Ferguson, the Gaelic-speaking Scottish Presbyterian minister who helped to introduce the concept to the fast-emerging era of modern capitalism, lived through the aftermath of Culloden. Ferguson witnessed the beginnings of the march of progress through his native Highlands, and, along with his famous contemporary Adam Smith, contributed to the intellectual life of the time. As the first thinker to "modernize" the idea of civil society, Ferguson is a prism through which the paradoxes and contradictions of civil society are reflected.

The professor of moral philosophy at the University of Edinburgh recognized in his *Essay on the History of Civil Society* that the march of progress and individual self-interest might pose problems for the world he saw unfolding as a result of new inventions, the expansion of Smith's division of labour (Ferguson called his era "the age of separations"), and the spread of industry. Throughout his *Essay*, Ferguson referred to this new order as a "polished society," which replaced the earlier, "rude" version. This age of separations, together with a centralized state, promised improvements in material life. But Ferguson also worried that it had a downside. "The separation of professions, while it seems to promise improvement of skill . . . serves, in some measure, to break the bands of society," he wrote. "The members of polished society are separated from each other, every individual is supposed to possess his species of talent, or his particular skill, in which the others are confessedly ignorant; and society is made to consist of parts, of which none is animated with the spirit of society itself."[4]

In his analysis of Ferguson's contribution to contemporary debates over the renovation and relevance of civil society, social theorist John Keane detects a thread connecting the eighteenth-century Scot to a dilemma persisting to this day. Keane argues that Ferguson recognized that the public spirit typical of clan (rude) societies he knew in the Scottish Highlands would only with very great difficulty be re-created in the far more complex, market-based societies of modern times, and that Ferguson implicitly (though tentatively) addresses important paradoxes: that the guarantee of human freedom requires a centralized state, but that those who exercise power in that state are likely to abuse it; and that ever more centralized and powerful manifestations of state and corporate power "break the bands of society" and undermine the citizens' capacity for independent associations.[5]

Ferguson's concerns for the social unity of the community will be familiar, then, to today's civil society advocates who worry about "bowling alone" and to communitarians who fret over the decline of the family.

The sceptical view of Ferguson and civil society in general would have it that the moral philosopher was a cat's paw for British imperialism and an apologist for a new capitalist order. Indeed, besides urging the Scottish troops in service to the English to maintain their loyalty to King George, Ferguson also went as an emissary for His Majesty's Government to negotiate with the American rebels at Philadelphia in 1778. What's more, he lived at a time when political representation in the polished society for which he stood excluded all men but property-holders as well as all women. When he was a professor, the entire burgh of Edinburgh had a grand total of thirty-three voters.[6] In his 1997 discussion of civil society, historian of Scots nationalism Tom Nairn is dismissive of the concept and its original Scottish exponent, suggesting that civil society as envisaged by Ferguson was limited: "Emancipation from tyranny was emphatically not intended to bestow citizenship upon the rabble." In ridiculing those who would argue that the post-Cold War years constitute an Age of Ascendant Civil Society, Nairn describes the concept as:

> the diffuse assemblage of anything and everything that can be located somewhere in between politics and state power on one hand, and the family on the other. So far, so banal: nobody would deny the existence or significance of such institutions, but in what sense do they compose an overall or corporate entity meriting a title like "civil society"? In what sense are they self-standing or self-directing as distinct from control by Monarchs, politicians, policemen or administrators? Much justified puzzlement has always surrounded the concept.[7]

This would seem to bring us back full circle to the description of civil society as conceptual ragbag. We find that those who make a living pondering such things as the relevance of civil society are divided on the usage of this old term. The concept is equally confounding for the average citizen who is not a scholar, policy entrepreneur, or NGO activist. Just what is the usefulness of such a term?

We are living in an era in which neo-liberal thinking dominates. Transnational capital holds sway. Workers, peasants, and indeed nation-states, we are told, have no choice but to compete or capitulate to these trends; the market can resolve public problems and even address global environmental and social justice issues.* In this context, it might seem that civil society has simply been captured by the dominant ideology, which stresses the need for private NGOs and ill-defined "communities" to look after public welfare and public provision. Or can the idea of civil society be usefully renovated to provide a way for the excluded to pry their way into a significantly different democratic space? With the end of bankrupt command socialism, with the apparent dominance of unfettered market capitalism opening up a yawning chasm of social inequality, and with the increasingly obvious frailty of a natural environment unable to cope with the onslaught of industrialism, our world has an obvious need for new analytical tools. We have to understand the thorny situation we face and seek new ways out of it. "Civil society" can be one—but only one—method of achieving these goals.

Civil society has always basically been a *reactive* idea. Most of the time those who have employed the term have been

---

* Of course, the ostensible impotence of government in the face of global capital is quickly put aside in the face of a Mexican or East Asian financial collapse, at which time national authorities are called in to bail out lenders and attempt to sort out market irrationalities.

reacting to despotism, and that despotism has most often taken the form of an authoritarian state. As Nairn puts it, thinkers from Adam Ferguson to Antonio Gramsci "have striven to describe civil society as an actual or possible state of affairs, a societal reality distinct from and independent of the state . . . an over-centralized, interfering, bureaucratically-organized and would-be omnipotent state . . . the Leviathan or great political monster."[8] From early modernity to fascist Italy and into our own era (postmodern, post-industrial, postcolonial, post-whatever), those who have mused about civil society have been reacting to the excesses of the state, the tendency of governments to push people around—or at least to fail to live up to their claims of representation.

Our own era, however, has seen the state fall into disrepute in part because of an attack by the ideologues of the free market. This is not to say that state despotism is not a threat, or that democratic victories over despotisms from South Africa to Poland, from Chile to Uganda, have been unimportant. But democracy, remember, is a historical project. It is coming "from those nights in Tiananmen Square," sings Leonard Cohen, who adds repeatedly in his chorus that democracy is also "coming to the U.S.A."[9] It is also something that people can approach, as Václav Havel reminds us, in the same way they move towards a distant horizon. USAID and the World Bank may concoct policy papers about pluralism and good governance, but democracy advances against despotism as citizens act politically, in the public sphere. As Douglas Lummis remarks, the concept of civil society "provides a space for public discourse, for the development of public values and public language."[10] The tension between despotism and democracy has no end, and civil society has an important role to play in the way that, say, People's Power contributed to the demise of the martial law regime of Ferdinand Marcos in the Philippines.

What can this concept offer in the face of an assault on the public sphere by the forces of the free market? Or capital in alliance with the state? Or the World Bank or the IMF in alliance with transnational corporations and the state? When this assault comes in the name of Progress? When capitalism (not to be confused with democracy) as a total social system generates as much poverty as wealth while simultaneously despoiling the natural environment? When the Narmada Dam threatens people and their common lands, which supposedly stand in the way of the scientific age and its supposedly higher stages of development? When private capital threatens public provision of health care while seeking to colonize the world's gene pool as part of a glowing new enterprise called biotechnology?

Big questions: to frame a response, let's return to the time of Adam Ferguson, when the forces of a self-regulating market were starting their offensive, enclosing common land and (often literally) harnessing children to the new technologies of the day. The industrial revolution and its accompanying global thrust for imperial power provoked an inevitable reaction. People rebelled against child labour and colonialism and, in time, these came to an end. This was Progress of a different sort. To be sure, new forms of domination appeared, taking their place alongside stubborn patriarchal and racial hierarchies. But as Karl Polanyi points out, the late nineteenth century and most of the twentieth witnessed a reaction as the forces of a self-regulating market (liberalism) suffered. At the same time, popular forces deployed the vocabulary of political liberalism to gain representation in government. Men without property and women secured the vote. It was all part of what Polanyi calls the "double movement":

> the action of two organizing principles in society, each of
> them setting itself specific institutional aims, having the

support of definite social forces and using its own distinctive methods. The one was the principle of economic liberalism, aiming at the establishment of a self-regulating market, relying on the support of the trading classes, and using largely *laissez-faire* and free trade as its methods; the other was the principle of social protection aiming at the conservation of man and nature as well as productive organization, relying on the varying support of those most immediately affected by the deleterious action of the market.[11]

Polanyi thought class was important. He emphasized that the reaction, the second part of his double movement, was animated by those who were getting shafted by economic liberalism and its "veritable faith in man's secular salvation through the self-regulating market."[12] That market, he argued, had an inevitable tendency to become "disembedded" from society and (in this he was a pioneer) the natural environment. Society and nature could only be safeguarded by social forces that were constantly defending people, land, and culture.

For Polanyi, the self-regulating market had an inevitable tendency to separate the economy from society, human society from the Earth. His "double movement" is the tension between the corrosive force of an unfettered free market and countervailing forces thrown up by society as people protect themselves and nature—what he referred to simply as the land. Polanyi did not hold up any hope that the command economy of state socialism would protect either the people or the land. The market had its role. Although he was not a Marxist, he did believe that if class struggle went beyond limited class interests to protect society's complex tapestry of culture, it could be an important part of his "Great Transformation."

Here was a thinker who recognized that what we now call "developed" societies could learn something from traditional societies. When Polanyi wrote in the 1940s, much of the world was still under formal colonialism. He saw the connection between the enclosure of common land in early modern Britain and the domination of "underdeveloped" societies by Europeans. He pointed out that "a League of Nations report mentioned with due horror the recent appearance of that ominous figure of the sixteenth century European scene, the 'masterless man' in the African bush." He was referring to the emergence of economic refugees, that class of people who even now, decades later, are swelling the slums of most Southern cities and are increasingly visible on the sidewalks of the North. Landless labourers were common to early modern Europe, in traditional societies whose social fabric was being ripped apart by colonialism and its intrusive market: "What the white man may still practice in remote regions today, namely, the smashing up of social structures in order to extract the element of labour from them, was done in the eighteenth century to white populations by white men for similar purposes."

The principle of freedom was as important to Polanyi as it has long been to liberals who speak of market freedom and democratic freedom. But he recognized that "noncontractual organizations of kinship, neighbourhood, profession and creed" in an important way represented a freedom that would have to be liquidated if economic liberals were to successfully integrate Southern societies into the global market, producing jute, tea, timber, whatever. Polanyi believed that Westerners had something to learn from communities (he sometimes called them "primitive") in which the individual "is not threatened by starvation unless the community as a whole is in a like predicament. . . . The principle of freedom from want was equally acknowledged in the Indian village community and, we might add, under almost every and any social organization up to about the beginning of sixteenth century Europe."[13]

Like other thinkers who react to the savage inequalities wrought by market society, Polanyi may gloss over various injustices of traditional and pre-feudal societies. Nonetheless, he was onto something that some advocates of civil society in our own time recognize, often only implicitly. It is this: Polanyi's "noncontractual organizations of kinship, neighbour-hood, profession and creed" are still with us today. Some people call them "civil society." These organizations are being threatened by market forces, as they were in colonial or early industrial times. Some of the people involved may retreat into ethnic sectarianism and racism, focusing their frustration on others who are poorer or weaker than they are, or who speak or look differently than they do. Civil society is no utopian moral space isolated from the contradictions, cruelties, and general messiness of politics. But other people are reacting, resisting globalization, resisting the notion that more freedom for investors somehow promotes the public good, that competition is the solution no matter what the problem. Here is Polanyi's "double movement" at work, the protection of society and nature from the market.

The defence of the Narmada River is one recent example of this double movement at work. The industrial variant of "development" threatened to destroy an indigenous homeland, with disastrous consequences for the natural environment. The thrust is driven from the top, with the backing of the state and international capital. Those most harmed react to protect themselves and their society, in this case in alliance with inter-national allies who share their alarm at the attack on their way of life. But this response does not come without local organizing and the mobilization of those most closely involved. It has been a decades-long struggle, with setbacks and victories. Only in recent years has it involved international alliances, overseas phone calls, and Internet organizing. When the police attacked the people's checkpoints in May 1998, word went out to the Save the Narmada group's wide network within a matter of hours. Such quick-response communication is just as useful for organizers as it is for writers, and it has helped activists from Amnesty International and Greenpeace to the Narmada Bachao Andolan.

In this respect, international solidarity in the era of globalization can take on novel forms. The speed of communication and new levels of cultural exchange allow people opposed to the diktat of the market or the heavy hand of the state—or both—to organize new alliances and mount twenty-first-century resistance campaigns. Certainly, the rise of a Global Civil Society armed with the speediest computers, capable of pushing fading nation-states around, is vastly overstated.* But nevertheless popular resistance is availing itself of some of the same networking tools that permit financiers to indulge in massive global currency speculation. The technology allows the international manifestations of social movements (environmental, feminist, peace, social justice) to campaign on issues from opposition to the Gulf War and curtailing the emission of greenhouse gases to the *fin de siècle* Jubilee 2000 campaign for Third World debt relief.

In 1998, for instance, a concerted international opposition campaign successfully derailed the efforts of international business and several of the world's most powerful governments to put into place a Multilateral Agreement on Investment (MAI). The agreement would have involved the nations of the Organization for Economic Co-operation and Development, most of the world's largest economies. Private business ("investors") would have had greater rights enshrined as part

---

* See, for instance, the argument made by Jessica Mathews, chapter 1, p.17.

of a formal treaty that would, opponents argued, erode national sovereignty and weaken the ability of citizens to influence decisions impinging on their lives. The anti-MAI forces focused their vociferous—and ultimately effective—campaign on corporate rights versus the rights of citizens and the nation-states that represent them. Citizens concerned about increasing corporate power in the global economy believe with good reason that they need some way to control (or at least regulate) multinational corporations and that the only way to exert such control is through the nation-state.

The agreement was finally scuttled when the French government indicated its opposition, followed closely by Australia. But although the MAI was defeated, its principles remain very much alive. There is little doubt that a similar treaty will resurface, perhaps at the World Trade Organization (WTO), perhaps elsewhere. And there is no doubt that the idea that the rights of corporations should be allowed to trump the rights of people to protect themselves, their cultures, and the natural environment will continue to provoke stiff opposition. When France's Ministry of the Economy, Finance, and Industry published its analysis of the demise of the MAI in late 1998, it indicated that the opposition it heeded was not made up solely of the traditional representatives of professions, unions, and economic institutions. Describing the strength of the reaction and the speed at which it developed as "surprising," the French government noted that NGOs played a pivotal role in organizing international opposition. Although it singled out environmental groups "in Anglo-Saxon countries," the French analysis made it clear that something broader was afoot, with "representatives of civil society" capable of instantaneous exchange of texts and sophisticated, informed critiques:

> The MAI . . . marks a step in international economic negotiations. For the first time, we are witnessing the emergence of

> a *"global civil society"* represented by non-governmental
> organizations, which are often active in several countries
> and communicate across international borders. This is no
> doubt an irreversible change. . . . The Agreement has
> become a symbol. It crystallizes civil society's objections to
> and frustrations with globalization. There is one central
> reason for this: the agreement is perceived as a threat to
> national sovereignty.[14]

What has traditionally been called international solidarity in
trade union and socialist circles means that people seek common ground that transcends faraway borders. These people
are to be found at the parallel conferences that inevitably
accompany official international gatherings: environmentalists
at the Rio Earth Summit; human rights activists at the Vienna
1993 World Conference on Human Rights; women at the 1995
Beijing conference; promoters of social justice at the UN's
1995 Copenhagen World Summit for Social Development.
Future ministerial meetings of the WTO will surely be shad-
owed by activists eager to lobby politicians and speak to the
press. If corporate libertarians can see the world as their oys-
ter, citizens and societies can do the same, making connections
to distant others, and acting on those connections.

In Canada a key organization in the anti-MAI mobilization
was the Council of Canadians. This politically non-partisan—
though distinctly political—organization grew from a few hundred members in 1985, when discussions of a free-trade agreement between Canada and the United States first began, to
one hundred thousand by 1998. Its biggest growth occurred in
1995 and 1996 during campaigns to protect social programs
and public pensions. It has fifty-five chapters of perhaps a
dozen activists each in cities across the country.[15] The Council
is a membership organization in name only, because most
members are simply financial supporters, not activists. Its

strength lies not in mobilizing people at the grassroots or on a national basis but in its ability to raise public issues through the media and its capacity to work with similar groups at home and abroad—publicizing, lobbying, networking. Its expenses are not underwritten by powerful corporations but by its mass membership. Donations are not tax-deductible. The Council, with its warnings about "corporate rule" and its defence of public provision, is an example of a new variant of civil society that would be instantly recognizable to Karl Polanyi as a countermovement seeking to protect society from the excesses of the market.

Although such groups try to persuade the public authorities to do this or not do that, their activities are often focused on the role of private business and the dangers of unregulated flows of capital. (David Korten, an activist-writer who had previously theorized about NGOs, titled a 1996 book *When Corporations Rule the World*.) What does it mean for giant communications firms like Germany's Bertelsmann AG to control so much book and magazine publishing, to say nothing of its interests in music? For Holland's Elsevier to dominate scholarly publishing? For Canada's Southam to control well over half the nation's newspapers? For Microsoft of the United States to so totally rule the world of computers? For Disney, Coke, and Colonel Sanders to so heavily influence popular conceptions of the good life?

For years questions of corporate clout have preoccupied citizens and governments, well before a wave of corporate mergers stunned the business world in 1998. Deutsche Bank AG, Germany's largest bank, acquired Bankers Trust Corp. of the United States to create the world's largest bank. The deal cost $10.1 billion. But huge as that seems, the merger paled beside other mergers and acquisitions that year. In the oil business Exxon acquired Mobil and BP joined with Amoco. In communications, Bell Atlantic got GTE, WorldCom got MCI Communications, AT&T got Tele-Communications, SBC Communications got Ameritech, Bertelsmann got Random House, Seagram got Polygram. In automobiles, Daimler-Benz hooked up with Chrysler. In the pharmaceutical-chemical sector, American Home Products acquired Monsanto. Many of these 1998 deals dwarfed the record 1996 purchase of Ciba-Geigy AG by Sandoz AG for $36.3 billion. Hundreds of billions of dollars changed hands. The sums involved were unimaginable—and incalculable because of the day-to-day volatility of stock markets.

The money that these corporations spent in acquiring each other could have been put to more mundane uses like feeding children, vaccinating poor people against preventable disease, or conducting research into energy production that does not threaten life on earth. After years of neo-liberal chatter about the dangers of intrusive government and the bankruptcy of the state, it is past time to face up to the power and priorities of this sort corporate *Anschluss*, the destabilizing role of capital in an increasingly unstable world economy.

The concerns of civil society—among them, of how citizens can best address the issues of feeding and caring for each other and the natural world—are clearly not the concerns of unfettered market forces that generate social disintegration and inequality. This thing called civil society, then, has a role in the protection of the public good, even if, again, it cannot automatically be assumed to be a Good Thing ("Look at all the thousands of community groups!") or looked on as a neo-liberal substitute for the state. As reactive and particular, civil society's natural focus is generally confined to the problems facing, say, a group of peasant women in rural Sri Lanka through Sarvodaya or the home care needs of Canada's frail elderly through the Victorian Order of Nurses. These projects are fine, but they do little by themselves to enable people— particularly the weakest members of society—to take more control over the decisions that have an impact on their lives, to protect themselves (and society) from a despotic state that has preoccupied so many civil society theorists and the market forces that so preoccupied Polanyi.

This sort of democratic impulse involves democratizing the market *and* the state. Democracy in this sense implies private citizens acting in public. It means self-government, democracy as a goal of human society, not simply a kind of government. This is where we can locate civil society as a space, separate from formal politics but very much politically engaged, where people act on issues that impinge on them directly or where they work to promote a more general public good. This sort of activity has contributed to the positive achievements of the past—the end of colonialism in the South and the public provision of universal health and education in the North. The right to vote, for both women and men. The right to freedom of association, to form unions, to speak freely without fear of arbitrary arrest. These things did not just happen, nor were they simply granted by the state and the powerful interests that tend to hold sway over government. They were the result of long, difficult campaigns by people trying to extend the idea of democracy, most often against the will of wealthy grandees of all kinds.

These efforts to broaden the idea of democracy and the realm of human freedom are played out in the space called civil society. They often involve a struggle over what might be called "common sense." Is it normal for women to have neither the vote nor any real control over their lives? For rulers to be able to jail and torture citizens with impunity? For the water we drink and the air we breathe to be treated like a common sewer? For some to have far too much while others starve? Clearly, disputes over what constitutes common sense involve political conflict, the challenge to things as they've usually been done.

Civil society is a geographically and socially uneven landscape, reflecting inequalities in society at large: landlords and landless labourers, financiers and slumdwellers, people of different religions or ethnic origins. It is and always will be contested terrain. It cannot be defined simply as a positive force, something that is good for democracy. Struggles that involve civil society are often political, promoting democracy in ways that do not simply involve control over the apparatus of the state. When people group themselves into associations aimed at, say, the preservation of customary rights to use forests or fishing grounds, saving them from destruction by outside contractors or foreign trawlers, they are promoting democracy to the extent that they are making an effort to govern or safeguard their own lives. But civil society organizations can also mobilize large numbers of supporters in the cause of religious fundamentalism or ethnic chauvinism, attacking people from other groups, burning their places of worship or neighbourhoods.

Jenny Pearce calls civil society an "arena of contestation," describing it as "a space which reflects the social divisions of society as a whole. To what extent the 'civil' or democratizing groups gain strength vis-a-vis opposing forces is part of the dynamics of history, to be researched and explained, not assumed."[16]

Civil society, then, is more than a throwaway term or a catchphrase. As a concept it can be a tool for social analysis, useful in tearing away stubborn old layers of common sense and crafting new ones. It is a very large tent, sheltering people and organizations that often have very little in common. Some of its practitioners challenge political despots or the let-the-market-decide status quo; others invariably defend inherited privilege and power. A key factor here is the success of classes or social movements in fashioning alliances, in persuading as many people as possible that a new way of seeing the world, an acceptance of a changed set of moral, political, or cultural values, makes common sense. Such projects are most successful when people—particularly people who have traditionally been excluded—imagine themselves as active participants in the making of their own history.

● ● ●

Civil society, it would seem, is a necessary but insufficient concept in the continuing project to expand democratic space, to make a difference in people's lives. A labourer in the Indian state of West Bengal made the point bluntly in his observations about changes that had come to his district: "It is a good thing that we are not beaten any longer and that we can tell them straight in the face things we don't like." Another Bengali man, the head of a family of nine who works as an agricultural labourer and a hawker while cultivating his own small plot of land, reflected much the same feeling. "We were really in a bind. Police would come and pester us," he recalled. "I tell you, we really suffered under the *zulum raj* [coercion] of those days. Nowadays, we can speak our own mind."[17]

In densely populated West Bengal, as Dutch anthropologist G.K. Lieten notes, "The public space . . . has increasingly been occupied by poor peasants and agricultural labourers."[18] The district is now apparently home to a general feeling that rice can be left outside, women can move around safely, and abuse of power by the authorities has disappeared. What's more, land reforms and a decentralization of power to local level village councils, *panchayats*, have weakened the influence of landlords over rural politics and economic conditions. Almost all the villagers agree that health conditions have improved, with paramedical workers making regular rounds. Social polarization has declined. The *panchayats* have been successful in attracting women to adult literacy classes. A measure of democracy characterizes local elections, which have high voter turnouts.

Since 1977 West Bengal has been administered by a Left Front government coalition dominated by the Communist Party of India. It may be the longest period of rule by democratically elected Marxists since the German philosopher began writing about class and class power over 150 years ago. Its control over state government has certainly not pleased everyone. Rich peasants and landlords have been displeased because the *panchayats* have instituted a system of voluntary labour that has resulted in major road improvements and all-season access to schools and hospitals. Those who do not wish to do road work, considering it beneath their dignity, must pay a levy in food, the amount calculated on the basis of land ownership. The main worry of the more affluent, however, is that labour is no longer as submissive as it once was. According to the richest peasant in one village, "The British period was the best; then came the Congress [Party] period."[19]

This is not to imply that all is rosy, that the changes are irreversible or that the *panchayat* system has not become bureaucratized or tinged with unfair practices. The government has lost influence in districts where it has become remote from its political base and when activists have misused power. But it is clear, concludes Lieten in his description of the view from below, that poor men and women are much more aware of what the public world is all about, and that they appear ready to intervene in that world to defend their rights.

All of which is a reminder that an effective associational revolution necessarily involves a collective action that crosses the shifting border between civil society and the public world—the world of politics and the state. Concrete, significant change requires grappling with political power to redistribute resources and put more control into the hands of people who have for centuries been excluded. But the paradox raised by civil society's theoretical vogue is that political power alone cannot bring about tangible change. Official Politics need to be supplemented by associational work—the organizing, the volunteering, the coalition-building, the construction of alternative institutions that contribute to Polanyi's double movement.

Throughout the South people are forced every day to deal with local "Big Men"—middlemen, landlords, moneylenders, party bosses, state apparatchiks. Sometimes these people confront power, often they simply have to cope by working around it, just as women—North and South—do in their dealings with men, both big and small. Throughout the North, citizens often deal with more subtle forms of power exercised in the mall, the mind, the market, the workplace. Throughout the world we all have to confront the way in which power is played out in this thing called civil society.

# Notes

## 1. Introduction: Unpacking the Conceptual Ragbag

1. United Nations Development Programme (UNDP), *Human Development Report 1996* (New York: Oxford University Press, 1996), p. 45; UNDP, *Human Development Report 1995* (New York: Oxford University Press, 1995), pp. 30-31; James Gustave Speth, "Foreword," UNDP, Human Development Report 1998 (New York: Oxford University Press, 1998), p. iii.
2. UNDP, *Human Development Report 1996*, p. 28.
3. The 1993 estimate was made by the Organization of European Co-operation and Development (OECD); data cited in D. Hulme and M. Edwards, "NGOs, States and Donors: An Overview," in *NGOs, States and Donors: Too Close for Comfort?* ed. D. Hulme and M. Edwards (Basingstoke: Macmillan, 1997), p. 6.
4. Jessica Mathews, "Power Shift," *Foreign Affairs*, vol.76, no.1 (January-February 1997); SAP Nepal, "Seminar on Decentralization and Civil Society for Participatory Development Process,"

mimeo, Kathmandu, 1997.

5.  Harvey Schachter, "A Question of Civility," *The Globe and Mail*, May 30, 1998, p. F1.

6.  United Nations, *The World Conferences: Developing Priorities for the 21st Century* (New York, 1997), p. v; emphasis added.

7.  Roy Trivedy and Jagabandhu Acharya, "Constructing the Case for an Alternative Framework for Understanding Civil Society, the State and the Role of NGOs," in *NGOs, Civil Society and the State: Building Democracy in Transitional Societies*, ed. A. Clayton (Oxford: INTRAC, 1996), p. 58.

8.  Murray Dobbin, *The Myth of the Good Corporate Citizen: Democracy under the Rule of Big Business* (Toronto: Stoddart, 1998), p. 167. For background on the BCNI, see pp. 165-81.

9.  L.R. Renshaw, "Strengthening Civil Society: The Role of NGOs," *Development*, 1994, p. 4.

10. See P.L. McCarney, ed., *The Changing Nature of Local Government in Developing Countries* (Toronto: Centre for Urban and Community Studies: Toronto, 1996), p. 11; cited in Steven Langdon, *Global Poverty, Democracy and North-South Change* (Toronto: Garamond Press, 1999), p. 176.

11. Jenny Pearce, "NGOs and Social Change: Agents or Facilitators?" *Development in Practice*, vol.3, no.3 (October 1993), pp. 225.

12. Lewis Perinbam, "Partners or Patrons?—Building New Relationships," notes for remarks to the SAP Annual Forum on Strengthening Civil Society, mimeo, Calgary, October 1997; emphasis in original.

13. Ostry quoted in Perinbam, "Partners or Patrons?"

14. Alan Fowler, "Strengthening Civil Society in Transition Economies," in *NGOs, Civil Society and the State*, ed. Clayton, p. 13.

15. G. Hansen, "Constituencies for Reform: Strategic Approaches for Donor-Supported Civic Advocacy Groups," in USAID Program and Operations Assessment, *Report*, no.12, 1996.

16. Benjamin Barber, *Jihad vs. McWorld: How Globalism and Tribalism Are Reshaping the World* (New York: Ballantine, 1995), p. 278.

17. Hansen, "Constituencies for Reform."

18. Douglas Lummis, *Radical Democracy* (Ithaca, N.Y.: Cornell

University Press, 1996), pp. 22, 31; emphasis added.

19. Ibid.

20. Neera Chandhoke, *State and Civil Society: Explorations in Political Theory* (New Delhi: Sage, 1995), pp. 34-35.

21. Quoted in Chandhoke, *State and Civil Society*, p. 38.

22. INTRAC, "Funding Development Organizations in the South: Strengthening Civil Society?" paper presented for workshop, Strengthening Civil Society: Progressive Strategy or Smokescreen? mimeo, Oxford, 1997.

23. Mathews, "Power Shift," pp. 63, 65.

24. Ibid., pp. 51, 52.

25. Jean Augustine, MP, to the annual meeting of Partnership Africa-Canada, September 1994, Hull, Quebec; quoted in David Sogge, "Settings and Choices," in *Compassion and Calculation: The Business of Private Foreign Aid*, ed. David Sogge (London: Pluto, 1996), p. 1.

26. Hulme and Edwards, "NGOs, States and Donors," p. 5.

27. Canadian Council for International Co-operation (CCIC), "What We Can Do: A 10-Point Agenda for Global Action against Poverty," Ottawa, 1997, p. 49.

28. Michael Walzer, "The Idea of Civil Society: A Path to Social Reconstruction," *Dissent*, Spring 1991, p. 293.

29. Trivedy and Acharya, "Constructing the Case for an Alternative Framework," p. 59.

30. Alan Fowler, "Civil Society and State Reform: Perspectives of a Positive Sceptic," *Global Alliance News*, March 1997, p. 8.

## 2. The Politics of Helping People: Canada and Sri Lanka

1. Sarah Jane Crowe, *Who Cares? The Crisis in Canadian Nursing* (Toronto: McClelland and Stewart, 1991), p. 49.

2. VON Canada, *A Century of Caring: The History of the Victorian Order of Nurses*, Ottawa, 1996, pp. 116, 102.

3. Ibid., p. 102.

4. Bill Gekoski, personal communication with author, Kingston, Ont., Feb. 4, 1998.

5. David J. Kettler, *The Social and Political Thought of Adam*

156  *Civil Society in Question*

*Ferguson* (Columbus: Ohio State University Press, 1965), pp. 44, 46, 49.

6. Quoted in V.K. Jayawardena, *The Rise of the Labour Movement in Ceylon* (Durham, N.C.: Duke University Press, 1972), p. 110.

7. E.F.C. Ludowyk, *The Modern History of Ceylon* (London: Weidenfeld and Nicholson, 1966), p. 204.

8. Ranjith Wanigaratne, "The State-NGO Relationship in Sri Lanka: *Rights, Interests and Accountability*," in *NGOs, States and Donors*, ed. Hulme and Edwards, p. 221.

9. Jean Perera et al., *A People's Movement under Seige* (Colombo, Sri Lanka: Sarvodaya, 1992), p. 140.

10. Jean Perera, "In Unequal Dialogue with Donors: The Experience of the Sarvodaya Shramadama Movement," in *NGOs, States and Donors*, ed. Hulme and Edwards, p. 158.

11. Perera et al., *People's Movement under Seige*, p. 138.

12. Perera, "In Unequal Dialogue with Donors," pp. 162-63.

13. Ian Smillie, *The Alms Bazaar: Altruism under Fire: Non-profit Organizations and International Development* (Ottawa: IDRC, 1995), p. 191.

14. Paul Harrison, *Inside the Third World*, 3rd ed. (Harmondsworth, England: Penguin, 1993), p. 345.

15. Satchi Ponnambalam, *Dependent Capitalism in Crisis: The Sri Lankan Economy 1948-1980* (London: Zed Press, 1980), p. 99.

16. Wanigaratne, "State-NGO Relationship in Sri Lanka," pp. 216-17.

17. Roland Hodson, "Elephant Loose in the Jungle: The World Bank and NGOs in Sri Lanka," in *NGOs, States and Donors*, ed. Hulme and Edwards, p. 170.

18. Perera, "In Unequal Dialogue with Donors," p. 160.

19. A.T. Ariyaratne, *Collected Works*, vol. 1 (Colombo: Sarvodaya, 1984); cited in Smillie, *Alms Bazaar*, p. 183.

20. Perera, "In Unequal Dialogue with Donors," pp. 165-67.

21. Wanigaratne, "State-NGO Relationship in Sri Lanka," pp. 226, 231.

22. Hodson, "Elephant Loose in the Jungle," p. 169.

23. Jørgen Lissner, "The Politics of Altruism," 1977, quoted in Smillie, *Alms Bazaar*, p. 36.

### 3. From Enlightenment to Globalization: A Historical Passage

1. Adam Smith, *Inquiry into the Nature and Causes of the Wealth of Nations*, Book I (New York: Everyman's Library, 1991), pp. 20-21.
2. Adam Smith, quoted in Chandhoke, *State and Civil Society*, pp. 97-98.
3. Roger Scruton, *A Dictionary of Political Thought* (London: Macmillan, 1982), p. 429.
4. Ibid.
5. Adam Ferguson, *An Essay on the History of Civil Society*, ed., with Introduction, by Duncan Forbes (Edinburgh: Edinburgh University Press, 1966), quoted in Tom Nairn, *Faces of Nationalism: Janus Revisited* (London: Verso, 1997), p. 75.
6. John Keane, "Despotism and Democracy: The Origins and Development of the Distinction between Civil Society and the State 1750-1850," in *Civil Society and the State*, ed. John Keane (London: Verso, 1988), pp. 40-41.
7. Ellen Meiksins Wood, "The Uses and Abuses of 'Civil Society,'" in *Socialist Register 1990*, ed. Ralph Miliband et al. (London: Merlin Press, 1990), pp. 60-61.
8. Lewis Mumford, *The City in History: Its Origins, Its Transformations and Its Prospects* (New York: Harcourt, Brace, 1961), pp. 446-47.
9. Chandhoke, *State and Civil Society*, p. 141.
10. Karl Marx, *Capital*, vol. 1, quoted in Chandhoke, *State and Civil Society*, pp. 141-42.
11. Quoted in Peter Marshall, *Demanding the Impossible: A History of Anarchism* (London: Fontana, 1993), p. 451.
12. Raymond Williams, *Keywords: A Vocabulary of Culture and Society* (London: Fontana, 1976), p. 145.
13. Chandhoke, *State and Civil Society*, pp. 148-49.
14. Ramesh Thakur, *The Government and Politics of India* (Basingstoke, England: Macmillan, 1995), quoted in Mike Mason, *Development and Disorder: A History of the Third World Since 1945* (Toronto: Between the Lines, 1996), p. 280.
15. Eric Hobsbawm, *Age of Extremes: The Short Twentieth Century*

(London: Abacus, 1995), p. 472.

16. Krishan Kumar, "Civil Society: An Inquiry into the Usefulness of an Historical Term," *British Journal of Sociology*, vol.44, no.3 (September 1993), p. 375. U.S. political theorist Michael Walzer credits East and Central Europeans with reviving the concept; see Walzer, "Idea of Civil Society."

17. Quoted in Michael Bernhard, *The Origins of Democratization in Poland: Workers, Intellectuals and Oppositional Politics, 1976-1980* (New York: Columbia University Press, 1993), p. 94.

18. Ibid., pp. 11-12.

19. Quoted in Z.A. Pelczynski, "Solidarity and 'The Rebirth of Civil Society' in Poland, 1976-81," in *Civil Society and the State,* ed. Keane, p. 361.

20. Quoted in Philip Thody, *Albert Camus, 1913-1960* (London: Hamish Hamilton, 1961), p. 203.

21. Hobsbawm, *Age of Extremes*, pp. 487, 489-90; emphasis in original.

22. Lester Salamon, "The Rise of the Nonprofit Sector," *Foreign Affairs*, vol.73, no.4 (July/August 1994), p. 109.

23. J. Rohwer, *Asia Rising*, New York, 1995, p. 261, quoted in Richard Smith, "Creative Destruction: Capitalist Development and China's Environment," *New Left Review*, March-April 1997, p. 5.

24. Merton Miller, quoted in *The New York Times*, Nov.14, 1993; Hobsbawm, *Age of Extremes*, p. 414.

25. Bell Northern Research, "The Power of a Global R&D Network," *Telesis*, no.99 (December 1994), p. 58.

26. Paul Hirst and Grahame Thompson, *Globalization in Question: The International Economy and the Possibilities of Governance* (Cambridge: Polity Press, 1996); see especially chapter 1.

27. Kofi Annan, "Message," in Canadian Council for International Co-operation, *What We Can Do: A 10-Point Agenda for Global Action against Poverty* (Ottawa: CCIC, 1998), p. 5; UNDP, *Human Development Report 1997* (New York: Oxford University Press, 1997), pp. 9, 27.

28. World Bank, *World Development Report*, 1991, cited in John Gaventa, "Poverty, Participation and Social Exclusion in North and South," *IDS Bulletin*, vol.29, no.1 (1998), p. 51.

29. Richard Barnet and John Cavanagh, *Global Dreams: Imperial Corporations and the New World Order* (New York: Touchstone, 1994), pp. 425-26.
30. Quoted in David R. Morrison, *Aid and Ebb Tide: A History of CIDA and Canadian Development Assistance* (Waterloo, Ont.: Wilfrid Laurier University Press, 1998), p. 38.
31. Keith Spicer, *A Samaritan State? External Aid in Canada's Foreign Policy* (Toronto: University of Toronto Press, 1966), pp. 249-50.

## 4. "As Long as People Are People": Voluntarism, Government, and Politics

1. Katherine Fierlbeck, *Globalizing Democracy: Power, Legitimacy, and the Interpretation of Democratic Ideas* (Manchester and New York: Manchester University Press, 1998), chapter 6, "Civil Society," pp. 147-73; originally presented as "Fetishizing Civil Society," annual meeting, Canadian Political Science Association, June 1996, p. 153.
2. Angus Reid, *Shakedown: How the New Economy Is Changing Our Lives* (Toronto: Doubleday, 1996), p. 19.
3. Canadian Association of Food Banks, *Hungercount '97*, 1997; cited in *CCPA Monitor* (Canadian Centre for Policy Alternatives, Ottawa), May 1998.
4. *CCPA Monitor*, June 1998, p. 15.
5. Pradeep Kumar, *From Uniformity to Divergence: Industrial Relations in Canada and the United States* (Kingston, Ont.: IRC Press/Queen's University, 1993), Table I, pp. 12-13.
6. Kevin Phillips, *The Politics of Rich and Poor: Wealth and the American Electorate in the Reagan Aftermath* (New York: Random House, 1990), p. 8.
7. Alan AtKisson, "Why Civil Society Will Save the World," in *Beyond Prince and Merchant: Citizen Participation and the Rise of Civil Society*, ed. John Burbidge (New York: Pact Publications, 1997), p. 290.
8. Hugh Segal, "Notes for an Address: Declaration of Candidacy for the Leadership of the Progressive Conservative Party of

Canada," Toronto, June 8, 1998.

9. Bob Rae, *The Three Questions: Prosperity and the Public Good* (Toronto: Viking, 1998), pp. 52-53.

10. *The Globe and Mail*, April 11, 1998.

11. E.P. Thompson, *The Making of the English Working Class* (Harmondsworth, England: Pelican, 1968), pp. 237-38.

12. Reid, *Shakedown*, pp. 265, 309.

13. Andrew Cohen, "How Ideology and Cynicism Poisoned U.S. Politics," *The Globe and Mail*, Dec. 19, 1998, pp. A1, A18.

14. Gaventa, "Poverty, Participation and Social Exclusion," pp. 50-51.

15. Williams, *Keywords*, p. 76.

16. Gregory Baum, "L'économie alternative," *Relations*, no. 548 (March 1989); quoted in Paul Leduc Browne, *Love in a Cold World? The Voluntary Sector in an Age of Cuts* (Ottawa: CCPA, 1996), p. 82.

17. Deena White, "The Community Management of Exclusion," translation, "La gestion communautaire de l'exclusion," *Lie Social et Politiques—RIAC*, no.32 (Fall 1994), pp. 1, 22-23.

18. David Sharpe, *A Portrait of Canada's Charities: The Size, Scope and Financing of Canada's Registered Charities* (Toronto: Canadian Centre for Philanthropy, 1994); cited in Jane Jenson and Susan Phillips, "Regime Shift: New Citizenship Practices for Canada," *International Journal of Canadian Studies*, Fall 1996.

19. Jenson and Phillips, "Regime Shift," pp. 111-35. Jenson and Phillips cite the work of Lester Salamon, a U.S. academic who has followed the development of his country's non-profit sector.

20. *Profile of a Changing World: 1996 Community Agency Survey* (Toronto: Municipality of Metropolitan Toronto, Social Planning Council of Metropolitan Toronto, City of Toronto, 1996), pp. 19, 46.

21. Tom Flanagan, "Social Services That Work," *The Globe and Mail*, Dec. 31, 1998, p. A19.

22. André Picard, "The Elusive Spirit of Giving," *The Globe and Mail*, Oct. 3, 1998, p. D2.

23. André Picard, "Profit in Giving," *The Toronto Star*, Nov. 16, 1997, citing data from Canadian Centre for Philanthropy.

24. Picard, "Profit in Giving."

25. Al Hatton, "Remarks to SAP Annual Forum: Strengthening Civil Society," mimeo, Ottawa, Oct. 3, 1997.

26. Jeremy Rifkin, *The End of Work* (New York: Tarcher/Putnam, 1995), p. 287.

27. The broad analysis that follows is taken from Susan Phillips, "Redefining Government Relationships with the Voluntary Sector: On Great Expectations and Sense and Sensibility," mimeo, discussion paper, Round Table on the Voluntary Sector, Ottawa, 1995, no pagination.

28. SJC-CFP, "Canada's Foreign Policy: Dissenting Opinions and Appendices," quoted in Morrison, *Aid and Ebb Tide*, p. 386.

29. "Reform Party Dissenting Opinion for the Standing Committee on Human Resources Development," quoted in Browne, *Love in a Cold World?* p. 19.

30. Browne, *Love in a Cold World?* pp. 46-47.

31. For a detailed overview of work time, increased time-squeeze, and income-polarization issues, see Human Resources Development Canada, *Report of the Advisory Group on Working Time and the Distribution of Work* (Ottawa: Minister of Supply and Services, 1994).

32. *The Toronto Star*, Nov. 16, 1997.

33. Sharpe, *Portrait of Canada's Charities*; cited in Browne, *Love in a Cold World?* p. 30.

34. Phillips, "Redefining Government Relationships," citing M. Hall and P. Reed, "Shifting the Burden: How Much Can Government Download to the Nonprofit Sector?" paper presented to ARNOVA Conference, Cleveland, 1995.

35. Fierlbeck, *Globalizing Democracy*, p. 157.

36. Robert Putnam, J-C. Casanova, and Seizaburo Sato, *Revitalizing Trilateral Democracies: A Report to the Trilateral Commission*, Trilateral Commission, 1995, p. 6.

37. Robert Bellah et al., *The Good Society* (New York: Knopf, 1991), pp. 49-50.

38. *The Globe and Mail*, Aug. 17, 1998.

39. E.J. Dionne, *Why Americans Hate Politics* (New York: Simon and Schuster, 1991), pp. 10-11. For the issue of poverty and voter registration in the United States, see Frances Fox Piven and Richard Cloward, *Why Americans Don't Vote* (New York:

Pantheon, 1989).

40. For details of California's decay, see Peter Schrag, *Paradise Lost: California's Experience, America's Future* (New York: The New Press, 1998).

41. Putnam, Casanova, and Sato, *Revitalizing Trilateral Democracies*, p. 71.

42. Milton Friedman and Rose Friedman, *Free to Choose: A Personal Statement* (New York: Harcourt Brace Jovanovich, 1980), p. 57.

43. Walzer, "Idea of Civil Society," p. 297.

44. Robert Putnam, *Making Democracy Work: Civic Traditions in Modern Italy* (Princeton, N.J.: Princeton University Press, 1993), pp. 167-75.

45. Robert Putnam, "Bowling Alone: America's Declining Social Capital," *Journal of Democracy*, vol.6, no.1 (January 1995), p. 65.

46. Ibid., p. 71.

47. Ibid., p. 69.

48. Ibid., p. 67.

49. Michael Foley and Bob Edwards, "The Paradox of Civil Society," *Journal of Democracy*, vol.7, no.3 (July 1996), pp. 36-52.

50. Charles Derber et al., *What's Left? Radical Politics in the Postcommunist Era* (Amherst: University of Massachusetts Press, 1995), p. 7.

51. Jean Cohen and Andrew Arato, *Civil Society and Political Theory* (Cambridge, Mass.: MIT Press, 1992), p. xii.

## 5.  Dams, Jeeps, and People-Centred Development: The South Asian Experience

1. Narmada Bachao Andolan, *Masheshwar Update*, May 20, 1998.

2. National Alliance of People's Movements, Bombay, 1996; quoted in Patrick McCully, *Silenced Rivers: The Ecology and Politics of Large Dams* (London: Zed Books, 1996), p. 306.

3. Narmada Bachao Andolan, *Victory at Masheshwar*, Feb. 3, 1998.

4. Quoted in Vidyut Joshi, *Submerging Villages: Problems and Prospects* (Dehli: Ajanta Publications, 1987), pp. i-ii.

5. Joshi, *Submerging Villages*, pp. 25-27.

6. Tom Athanasiou, *Divided Planet: The Ecology of Rich and Poor* (Boston: Little, Brown, 1996), p. 204.

7. *The Los Angeles Times*, Feb. 6, 1995; quoted in McCully, *Silenced Rivers*, p. 240.

8. Lewis Mumford, *The Myth of the Machine: The Pentagon of Power* (New York: Harcourt, Brace, 1964), p. 128.

9. Harry Truman, "Inaugural Address," 1949, quoted in Lummis, *Radical Democracy*, p. 58.

10. See Rajesh Tandon, "Local Governance, Democratic Transition and Voluntary Development Organizations: Some Lessons from South Asia," in *NGOs, Civil Society and the State*, ed. Clayton.

11. Lisa Jordan and Peter van Tuijl, "Political Responsibility in NGO Advocacy: Exploring Emerging Shapes of Global Democracy," mimeo, 1997, no pagination.

12. Edward Said, *Culture and Imperialism* (New York: Vintage, 1994), p. 25.

13. Rohit Kumar Nepali, *Civil Society: Voice to the Powerless People* (Kathmandu: South Asia Partnership-Nepal, 1997), p. 5.

14. SAP Nepal, "Seminar on Decentralization and Civil Society," p. 3.

15. Nanda Shrestha, "Becoming a Development Category," in *The Power of Development*, ed. J. Crush (London: Routledge, 1995), pp. 274-75, 277, 272.

16. Nepali, *Civil Society*, p. 17.

17. G. Upreti et al., "Nepal," in *The Dispossessed: Victims of Development in Asia*, ed. V. Raina et al. (Hong Kong: Arena Press, 1997), pp. 257-73.

18. Nepali, *Civil Society*.

19. Jordan and van Tuijl, "Political Responsibility in NGO Advocacy."

20. Sogge, "Settings and Choices," p. 12.

21. Mohammad Tahseen, *Civil Society Organizations in Pakistan: A Situation Analysis* (Lahore: SAP Pakistan, 1997), p. 5.

22. Ibid., pp. 2, 6.

23. Iftikhar Malik, *State and Civil Society in Pakistan* (London: Macmillan, 1997), quoted in Mohammad Qadeer, "The Evolution of Civil Society and Social Transformation in Pakistan," paper presented to Pakistan Society of Development Economists, annual meeting, 1997.

24. Qadeer, "Evolution of Civil Society," p. 8.
25. Carlos M. Vilas, "The Hour of Civil Society," *NACLA Report on the Americas*, vol.27, no.2 (1993).
26. Quoted in Paikiasothy Saravanamuttu, "Sri Lanka: Civil Society, the Nation and the State-building Challenge," in *Civil Society and the Aid Industry: The Politics and Promise,* ed. Alison Van Rooy (London: Earthscan, 1998), p. 112.
27. Ibid., pp. 116-17.
28. Ibid.
29. Hodson, "Elephant Loose in the Jungle," p. 169.
30. Ibid., pp. 185, 181.
31. Ibid., p. 118.
32. Philip Biswas, "Civil Society in Bangladesh," mimeo, Jessor, Bangladesh, Oct. 27, 1997.
33. Faris Ahmed, *In Defence of Land and Livelihood: Coastal Communities and the Shrimp Industry in Asia* (Ottawa: CUSO, Inter Pares, Sierra Club of Canada, Consumers' Association of Penang, 1997), p. 14.
34. See Ahmed, *In Defence of Land and Livelihood*, p. 30. The following information on shrimp acquaculture in Bangladesh draws from this study.
35. Biswas, "Civil Society in Bangladesh."
36. Ibid.
37. Philip Biswas, "A Brief Scenario on Bangladesh Situation," e-mail from SAP/Ottawa, 1997.
38. Hulme and Edwards, "NGOs, States and Donors," pp. 9-10.
39. Aparna Sundar, "Sea Changes: Organizing around the Fishery in a South Indian Community," Ph.D. thesis (pending), Department of Political Science, University of Toronto.

## 6. Conclusion: Towards the "Double Movement"

1. John Prebble, *Culloden* (Harmondsworth, England: Penguin, 1961), p. 10.
2. Nairn, *Faces of Nationalism*, p. 77.
3. Michael Lynch, *Scotland: A New History* (London: Pimlico, 1991), pp. 369, 386.

4. Ferguson, *Essay on the History of Civil Society*, p. 218.
5. Keane, "Despotism and Democracy," p. 43.
6. Lynch, *Scotland*, p. 386.
7. Nairn, *Faces of Nationalism*, pp. 80, 77.
8. Ibid., p. 75.
9. Leonard Cohen, "Democracy," Stranger Music Inc. (BMI), 1992.
10. Lummis, *Radical Democracy*, p. 31.
11. Karl Polanyi, *The Great Transformation: The Political and Economic Origins of Our Time* (Boston: Beacon Press, 1957), p. 132.
12. Ibid., p. 135.
13. Ibid., pp. 163-64.
14. Catherine Lalumière and Jean-Pierre Landau, *Report on the Multilateral Agreement on Investment* (Paris: Ministry of the Economy, Finance and Industry, 1998), p. 4.
15. John Urquhart, Council of Canadians, Ottawa, personal communication with author, Dec. 3, 1998.
16. Jenny Pearce, "Civil Society, the Market and Democracy in Latin America," *Democratization*, vol.4, no.2 (1997), p. 72.
17. Quoted in G.K. Lieten, "Rural Development in West Bengal: Views from Below," *Journal of Contemporary Asia*, vol.24, no.4 (1994), pp. 524, 526.
18. Ibid., p. 516.
19. Quoted in ibid., pp. 519-20.

# Index

Aberdeen, Lady Ishbel 24
Acharya, Jagabandhu 6-7
Acres Consulting (Canada) 103
Agarwaal, Alok 100
Amnesty International 4, 142
Annan, Kofi 6, 62
Arato, Andrew 98
Ariyaratne, A.T. 31-32, 33, 36, 37
Arun Dam project (Nepal) 110-11
Asea Brown Boveri 101, 117
AtKisson, Alan 67-68
Ayub Khan, Mohammad 114

Bangladesh 1, 121-26
Bangladesh Rural Advancement
    Committee (BRAC) 19, 124-26
Baum, Gregory 73
Bhutto, Zulfikar 114
Billah, Robert 89
Billett, Murray 68
Bonnah, Cathy 26
bowling 93, 94
Boy Scouts 51, 93
Business Council on National Issues
    (BCNI) 6, 7
business unionism 96

Canada 9; UN ranking of 2; NGOs in
    3-4, 20; civil society in 6-7, 69-
    88; voluntary sector in 74-78
Canadian Council for International
    Co-operation (CCIC) 20
Canadian International Development
    Agency (CIDA) 4, 33, 80
Canadian Radio-television and
    Telecommunications
    Commission 80
capitalism 41-51, 134-35
CARE 6, 18, 19, 20
Ceylon. See Sri Lanka.
CIVICUS 71
Chandhoke, Neera 5, 15, 47, 50
China 57, 58-59, 103
churches. See religion and religious

organizations.
civil society, composition of 6-8, 16;
    defined 4-5, 6, 8, 21-22;
    "global" 17-18, 142-44; modern
    emergence of 29-30, 41-46, 133-
    35; and traditional societies 30,
    44, 51, 107-8, 114, 132; and
    contracting regime 33-34, 73-78;
    re-emergence of 51-58; popular-
    ity of 67-68; as reactive idea
    136-44; nature of 148-49
Clinton, Bill 71, 93
Coalition for Better Childcare 87
CoDevelopment Canada 20
Cohen, Jean 98
Cold War 53, 55, 59, 65-66
colonialism 2, 49, 139-40; in Ceylon
    30-31; disrupts social relations
    51; breakup of 52-53; in India
    101, 132-33; legacy of 106-7
communications technology 17, 100,
    141-42, 143-44
communitarianism 11
community 9, and funding 38-39; as a
    notion and force 72-78, 126-27,
    136
Conference on Environment and
    Development (UN). See Rio
    Summit.
consumerism 2, 59, 108
Council of Canadians 144-45
Culloden, Battle of 131-32, 133
CUSO 6, 9
Czechoslovakia 56-57

dam projects 64, 99-105, 110-11
democracy 12-14, 45; "of unfreedom"
    47; revisioning of 56; in Canada
    70-71; and civil society 92-98,
    117; and Pakistan 115; as an
    ideal or historical project 128,
    137-38; broadening of 147-49
development 1-3; growth theory 12;
    Western model rejected 32;

167

clash of approaches 36; participatory 36, 38; and Cold War 58-
59; in postcolonial era 104-5;
and indigenous cultures 108-13;
and traditional societies 139-41.
*See also* foreign aid.
Donner Foundation 76

East Germany 56
*The Economist* 4, 54, 59
Edwards, Michael 125-26
environmental issues 48, 103, 109-10,
123, 139-42
exclusion 72

Ferguson, Adam 14, 29-30, 43-44, 45,
51, 71, 133-35, 137, 138
Fierlbeck, Katherine 65-66, 87-88
fisheries 122-24, 126-27
food banks 66-67
Fordism 95
foreign aid 3, 9, 10-14, 20, 33-34, 59,
64, 107-12
Fowler, Alan, 11, 21
France 132, 143-44
Fraser Institute 76-77
Friedman, Milton 91, 92
Fukuyama, Francis 68

Gandhi, Mohandas Karamchand 1,
32
Gekoski, Bill, 28
globalization 48, 58-64, 92, 95-96,
101, 109
Goldsmith, Oliver 69
Grameen Bank 124-25
Gramsci, Antonio 15, 49-52, 71, 107,
128, 137
Greenpeace 18, 94, 142

Harmston, Richard 21-22
Hatton, Al 78-79
Havel, Václav 65, 128, 137
hegemony 49, 50
Hirst, Paul 61
Hobsbawm, Eric 57-58, 60
Horizons of Friendship 3
Hulme, David 125-26

Hungary 56

Illich, Ivan 60
India 53-54, 60, 95, 99-106, 126-27,
133, 140, 149-51
interest groups 8, 80-81
International Monetary Fund (IMF)
54, 138
International Network Against
Unsustainable Aquaculture 124
International Non-governmental
Organization Training and
Research Centre (INTRAC) 16
Ip, Ivan 26-27
Italy 92

Jacobite rebellion 131-33
Janasaviya Trust Fund (JTF, Sri
Lanka) 120
Jenson, Jane 75-76

Keane, John, 44-45, 134
Keynes, John Maynard 52-53
Keynesianism 54-55, 62, 70
Kinsmen Club 28
KOR (Workers' Defence Committee,
Poland) 56
Kuron, Jacek, 56

labour movement 26-28, 31, 50, 56,
67, 94-95
League of Women Voters (U.S.) 93
Lenin, V.I. 48-49, 57
Lieten, G.K. 149, 151
Lions Club 77
Li Peng 103
Locke, John 66, 90
Lummis, Douglas 14, 137

Malatesta, Enrico 49
Marcos, Ferdinand 137
Mathews, Jessica 17-18, 142
market economy/forces 13, 16, 52,
95; and contracting 25, 27, 73-
78; and development 41-43;
global reach of 47-48; and consumer choice 59; tendency to
overcapacity 63; as distinct from